V. I. LENIN

MODERN MASTERS

Already published

ALBERT CAMUS / Conor Cruise O'Brien
FRANTZ FANON / David Caute
HERBERT MARCUSE / Alasdair MacIntyre
CHE GUEVARA / Andrew Sinclair
CLAUDE LÉVI-STRAUSS / Edmund Leach
LUDWIG WITTGENSTEIN / David Pears
GEORGE LUKÁCS / George Lichtheim
NOAM CHOMSKY / John Lyons
JAMES JOYCE / John Gross
MARSHALL MCLUHAN / Jonathan Miller
GEORGE ORWELL / Raymond Williams
SIGMUND FREUD / Richard Wollheim
WILLIAM BUTLER YEATS /
  Denis Donoghue
WILHELM REICH / Charles Rycroft
MOHANDAS GANDHI / George Woodcock
BERTRAND RUSSELL / A. J. Ayer
NORMAN MAILER / Richard Poirier

MODERN MASTERS

EDITED BY frank kermode

v. i.
lenin

robert conquest

NEW YORK | THE VIKING PRESS

FOR ARNOLD BEICHMAN

CONTENTS

Introduction

Of all the figures dealt with in this series, it will hardly be denied that by far the biggest shadow is cast by Lenin. At least, this is true if we consider the political and social world, for it might be argued that in some long run a writer like Camus or a philosopher like Wittgenstein would endure even better. But Frantz Fanon or Che Guevara (as they would themselves, of course, have readily conceded) shrink to almost nothing compared with the man who created a centralized revolutionary party machine, with it took and held power over a major country, and founded and inspired a similar set of parties with similar aims throughout the world.

Nor is the power of his teaching and of his example spent. With the exception of anarchists (who have from the start condemned his whole record) there are few revolutionaries in the world who are not, or do not believe themselves to be, in some sense "Leninist." The same applies to the rulers, however mutually antipathetic, of the whole range of Communist states from Cuba to China, from Russia to Yugoslavia.

But the center from which this whole movement spread was Russia, and within Russia the Bolshevik Party, and within the Bolshevik Party Lenin. The extent to which the will power and the conceptions of the single individual Lenin dominated the whole course of events in Russia is astounding—particularly perhaps to believers in the decisive role of social power and disbelievers in historical accident.

If Lenin had died young, the tightly centralized Bolshevik Party could scarcely have emerged. If he had dropped dead in Zurich in March 1917, the Bolsheviks would not have moved into a position of total hostility to the other socialist and democratic parties. If he had died in July or August 1917, they would not have seized power. If he had died in early 1918, they would not have signed the Treaty of Brest-Litovsk, and would have fallen. If he had died under Fanny Kaplan's bullets in August 1918, they would most probably have lost the Civil War. But for his insistence they would almost certainly not have switched to the New Economic Policy in 1921, and this would probably have meant their collapse. But for his survival to introduce the surprise resolution at the Tenth Party Congress suppressing organized opposition in the Party, Russia might not have been thrown into the hands of Stalin and the Party apparatus. And, but for his insistence, the Communist International might not have been formed and, if it had been, would at any rate scarcely have been turned (by the "Twenty-one Conditions") into a centralized array of parties on the precise Bolshevik model.

None of this is normally disputed by friend or foe. It amounts to saying that but for Lenin, the monolithic party would not have arisen, would not have come to power, would not have survived if it had, and would not have been a pattern for similar parties throughout the world. Whatever view one takes of the desirability or otherwise of what actually happened as a result of his political career, it is clear that the world has been changed by it on a large scale and in a decisive manner.

More has probably been written about Lenin than about any other figure of this century. Many and varied opinions of him have been and are still current. At the time of the Bolshevik Revolution he was, for very many people, a monster thrown up from nowhere amidst the chaotic disintegration of a barbaric society. For a minority of socialists and others, he was a proletarian democrat, speaking the accustomed language of European Marxism.

Then, when he died, and the regime settled down to become accepted, if not loved, abroad, a certain blunting of the acerbities took place, at least as regarded the man himself. (His successor helped too: compared with Stalin's, anyone's rule would appear in retrospect as a veritable Arcadia.) Moreover Leninists in Russia and outside, were powerful and persistent in speech and print. History, we are told, is the propaganda of the victor. Lenin's works attacking his critics appeared everywhere: their answers were forgotten. In London, a Little Lenin Library was published, but not even a Minor Martov Memoir. For of course that time it was mainly the revolutionary left that was interested. At that time few others, and fewer scholars, were equipped to study Lenin or his career.

Lately, especially in the past couple of decades, a formidable body of research has at last, in almost all cases, separated the facts from the incrustations of legend. Facts are, of course, presented for judgment, and various judgments are possible. But at least the evidence is now reliable, and today, just over a hundred years after his birth, we are probably in as good a position as we are likely to find, until the passing of centuries establishes a fuller perspective, to form a balanced view of his career and his ideas.

Lenin took power in the name of an idea. But, as

Marx tells us of earlier movements, the ideas in the minds of political leaders are often distorted representations of the social and other forces involved. It is not what they think they are doing, but what they are actually doing that matters.

His impact upon the world was not, generally speaking, that of a theoretician. His main amendments to or "creative developments" of orthodox Marxism are, first, a return to a rather pre-Marxist emphasis on the role of an organized political elite as against that of the proletariat, or, as E. H. Carr has put it, "the substitution of party for class as the motive force of revolution"; and second (and less distinctively, since other prominent Social Democrats had produced earlier analyses), his theory of the "imperialist" phase of capitalism.

But the power and influence of all such writings have arisen largely from the fact that the author himself carried out a major revolution. The prestige of his actions validated his works. Lenin is, in fact, one of those masters who can be meaningfully presented only in more or less biographical and historical form. In so doing in the following pages, however, my aim is neither biographical perspective nor historical completeness as such, but rather to give, as clearly as may be, a picture of Lenin, the political animal, in action and thought.

Background and Evolution

1

Vladimir Ilyich Ulyanov, later to be known as Lenin, was born on April 22, 1870, in the town of Simbirsk, on the Volga. Simbirsk lies in an area where the European and Asiatic cultures meet, and more than a third of the provincial population were non-Russians. Kazan, a couple of hundred miles to the north, where Lenin went to university and later lived on his mother's nearby family estate, was the cultural capital of the Muslim Tatars. In fact, this is the northern sector of that extreme periphery of old Christendom where, from the Urals through Armenia and "Chaldea" to Ethiopia, strange sects and heresies have traditionally had their being.

But Lenin's family provided a Europeanizing and civilizing ambiance. He was the second son, and third child, of Ilya Nikolaevich Ulyanov and his wife Maria, née Blank.

Lenin's paternal grandfather Nikolai was a serf who learned a craft and bought his freedom. His wife Anna was a Kalmyk. His son, Lenin's father, born in 1831, graduated from high school in 1850, went to university, and became a physics and mathematics teacher. He was a great admirer of Tsar Alexander II and a loyal public servant, orthodox in religion and devoted to improving his country by education. He eventually rose to be director of schools in the Simbirsk province—with a civil-service rank equivalent to major general—hence to the hereditary nobility. (Social mobility under the autocracy was surprisingly great. The White Commander-in-Chief in the Civil War, General Anton Denikin, was the son of a serf, and Lavr Kornilov, the "reactionary" leader in 1917, came up from poverty. But this only partially parallels anything in the West. It may be thought to be a mobility more like that found in an Oriental despotism, where a slave could become grand vizier, or the early Roman Empire, where a freedman could rise to power.)

Lenin later bitterly condemned the common transformation of radical and socialist intellectuals into loyal functionaries of the government who justified themselves by their "utility" within the limits of their job. Trotsky comments that these words could, after all, not be applied to Ilya Ulyanov, since he had never been any sort of radical; he was, in fact, conservative, though not reactionary. And Lenin remained a devoted son: there are few hints of rebellion against, or resentment at, his father.

In 1863 Ilya married Maria Alexandrovna Blank. Her father, Alexander Blank, was a doctor and also owned a small estate at Kokushkino in the Kazan province, where he was enrolled in the list of landed gentry. At one time in Lenin's youth the family lived on this maternal estate, and he later used occasionally to say to Party associates, "I, too, am a squire's child"; he always spoke nostalgically, and without political and social sneers, of life on the manor. There have lately been suggestions, not yet properly substantiated, that Dr. Blank was of Jewish origin,[1] but converted to Orthodoxy. His wife was a Volga German and a Lutheran.

In any case, their daughter Maria, Lenin's mother, ran her household in the German Protestant manner. An orderliness, diligence, and lack of demonstrativeness uncommon in the truly Russian family prevailed.

Lenin's diverse racial origins had little conscious significance to himself. Though totally lacking in racial chauvinism, he was always very much the product of the Russia of his time and in spite of an education in Western thought always saw the rest of the world through Russian eyes. (In a year in London he never went to a Labour meeting; in two years in Cracow he learned no Polish.) All the same, we may perhaps see the origins of his life style, so different from that of most Russians (and especially most Russian intellectuals), in this background. Vera Zasulich, the famous ex-terrorist who was one of Lenin's closest Social Democratic collaborators at the turn of the century and went on to become a Menshevik, always called him "Herr Doktor" or "Herr Professor" and said that his orderly and hard-working life, so different from that of most émigrés, spoke of his German origins. Others called him simply "the German"— not because they knew or cared about his maternal ancestry but as tribute, however oblique, to his undistractable devotion to his tasks.

Men are the products of their environment, as Marxists are the first to insist. There were many young men from the same environment as Lenin, and only one Lenin. Indeed, Lenin's own brothers, and sisters too, became revolutionaries, but they did not become Lenins. Still, that background—or the particular selec-

---

[1] If so, it is interesting that three out of Lenin's four grandparents were of nationalities specially persecuted by the Soviet authorities in the 1940s and later.

tion from it made for him by his temperament—can
hardly be dismissed.

The Russia in which he and his ideas evolved had a
social order, and a history, very different from those of
the West. This has to some extent been obscured by an
overschematic use of such general concepts as "feudalism." But, at any rate since Mongol times, Russian
"feudalism" (if we are to use the word) was of a nature
totally unlike that of the West. In Britain it sprang
up as a system of mutual obligations, in which the
legal and constitutional side became more and more
clearly defined until, half a millennium ago, serfdom
petered out. In Russia, movement was in the other direction: serfdom came in gradually, and was fully established only in the seventeenth century. The motive was
to bring the huge and expanding territories of the new
Muscovite empire under the firm control of the state.
"The state swelled up; the people shrank." The costs of
the imperial bureaucracy and army were always too
great for the country's economy—as they still are.

More important still, there was no question of the
Western system of mutual rights and obligations. Everyone was, in principle, simply the servant of the autocrat.

Throughout Russian history, the country was admin-
istered by a stratum which in return was rewarded not
only with payment but also with special rights withheld
from everyone else. It was always a "privilegentsia." In a
sense, as Professor Richard Pipes has remarked,
"Because of the traditionally close relationships between
government and its service class, Russia, past and present
alike, fits better the Marxist model of a class society
than does any other European country."

The "modernization" carried out by Peter the Great
and Catherine the Great consisted of the rationalization
of this system and the establishment in Russia of the
technical, military, and administrative methods of the
West, but nothing of its civic and political content. At
the beginning of the nineteenth century most of the

population were "serfs." (This word is to a great degree misleading. The usual Russian word *"rab"* means slave. And in fact the serf had if anything fewer rights than the slaves of the Americas.) Russia was thus afflicted at the top by the irresponsibilities of absolute power, and at the base by the absence of social responsibilities and rights.

In the nineteenth century, however, the beginnings of a great change began to show themselves. Western ideas came back with the officers who had defeated Napoleon, Tsar Alexander II emancipated the serfs in 1861, and through the century there arose an educated middle class, even though it largely lacked both civic experience and general self-confidence.

Boris Pasternak several times wrote of the evolution of Russia in the nineteenth century, and made it the theme of his uncompleted last work, his play *The Blind Beauty*. His interpretation was that, in the 1840s serfdom was obsolete, yet no tangible hope was to be seen; in the 1860s "liberal landowners have appeared and the best among Russian aristocrats began to be deeply stirred by Western ideas"; and finally in the 1880s came "the birth of an enlightened and affluent middle class, open to Occidental influences, progressive, intelligent, artistic."

The birth, yes. But at this stage it was far from being a decisive element in Russian life. And there were periods of progress and periods of reaction. Nevertheless the influence of its ideas penetrated the Russian political scene and had to be taken into account by the bureaucrats and autocrats. Its achievement was, above all, the Russian Enlightenment, whose principles have ever since remained in being in Russia, however much silenced and suppressed, right up to the present day.

But the temperament of people who have never known the efficacy of political evolution is likely to produce currents hostile to such gradual and uncertain improvement. Against the liberals who sought to humanize the autocracy on the basis of the natural movements of education, economics, culture, and power, the absolutist, moralist revolt of detesters of compromise came into being. The liberal, who wanted no more than the traditional liberties of the West, won the contempt of those who noted the slowness and setbacks of the constitutional struggle and who saw their task, in any case, as the creation not merely of a better but of a perfect society.

The atmosphere in revolutionary circles is best known to us, from two different points of view, in Dostoevski's *The Possessed* and Turgenev's *Fathers and Sons*. But this extremism was not a mere generational response of the 1860s. Even among the Decembrists of the 1820s Pavel Pestel had worked out a form of state which amounted to Utopia enforced by centralized terror. And, as the century goes on, we find what appear to be many such anticipators of Lenin's concepts—but theirs are, of course, to put it more rationally, the ideas on which Lenin drew.

Already in the 1860s, P.N. Tkachev, a strong proponent of the rights of the intellectual minority in view of "its higher mental and moral development," noted that time in Russia was not on the side of the revolution: the growth of capitalism would bring bourgeois values and general moderation. As we shall see, this idea was important in the creation of "Leninism" at the turn of the century, as against the general Marxist concepts Lenin had meanwhile absorbed.

Tkachev also commented that it was, in another sense too, much to Russia's advantage that there was no strong middle class, since this meant that the social order was held together only by the police and the army. What was necessary to break it? "Not much: two or three military defeats . . . some peasant uprisings . . . open revolt in the capital. . . ."

Again, Peter Zaichnevsky summed up the revolutionary elitist position in 1862: "We are firmly convinced that the revolutionary party, which will become the government, if the attempt be successful, ought to preserve its present centralization . . . in order to introduce new foundations of economic and social life in the shortest possible time. It should seize dictatorial powers and not refrain from taking any necessary steps. The elections to the National Assembly should take place under the influence of the government, which will make sure that it will not contain the partisans of the old order (should they remain alive). . . ."

Above all there was Nikolai Chernyshevsky, "the prophet of populist ideology," from whom Lenin took his first revolutionary ideas and whose influence he was to admit and praise throughout his career. Chernyshevsky's "novel," *What Is to Be Done?* published in 1863, was intended as a reply to *Fathers and Sons*. Though, as a novel, it has often been described as one of the very worst in all literature,[2] as a political pamphlet it had enormous influence. Chernyshevsky stood for a conscious devoted elite of revolutionary intellectuals, and above all for a hatred of liberals and liberalism.

There are certain periods, certain countries and cultures, in which the intolerant hostility prevailing between the holders of different ideas is of such a nature as to be barely comprehensible to those living in easier-going conditions. The theological hatreds of fourth-century Alexandria or of seventeenth-century Massachusetts are barely comprehensible to a John Stuart Mill or a Walter Bagehot. But anyone who reads the Russian intellectuals, Marxist or non-Marxist, of around the turn of the century must be struck by a similar spirit. Nikolai Berdyaev explains that the "intolerance of the Russian intelligentsia was self-protective; only so could it preserve itself in a hostile world; only thanks to

---

[2] It is an interesting fact that, apart from Alexander Herzen, virtually none of the vast literary talent in Russia at this time was in the revolutionary camp; it was either liberal or reactionary or quietist.

fanaticism could it weather persecution." (One result of the *odium theologicum* which thus flourished was to be the constant appeal by each contestant in a heresy or schism to the mere texts of Marx—as nowadays, of course, of Lenin.)

The Russian revolutionary intelligentsia was a most peculiar milieu. Its qualifications did not come from a man's origins, or his profession. One might be of noble birth, one might be rich. One did not even need to practice inverted snobbery and conceal or repudiate such things. So long as one believed in and devoted one's life to the ideas—in fact, the Idea—of the milieu, one was an *intelligent*. And Lenin's complete lack of the acquisitive urge too was not specifically a product of socialist principles but was shared by practically all the Russian intelligentsia.

On the other hand, in the interests of his overriding political certitudes, Lenin had a deep detestation of much that he saw among Russian intellectuals, and he was always attacking the intelligentsia in general in the most withering terms, as "wets" and so forth. He objected particularly to their constant appeal to moral principles, contrary to his own view that political interest invariably transcended such. Moreover, he had no trace of self-pity or of that glorying in defeat and persecution which marked an important section of the intelligentsia.

While he was still a schoolboy, a further evolution was taking place. The ideas of the pioneer revolutionaries were spreading to wider circles. The ideas of the European socialist and anarchist thinkers percolated into the movement, Marx's important among them. But as a significant political phenomenon Russian revolutionary activity and organization can be said to start with the Populists—the Narodniks. The first phase in the early 1870s saw these largely intellectual groups "Going to the People," in the hope of rousing the peasantry in their favor. The total failure of this campaign led to the turning of the "People's Will" intellectuals to individual terror, culminating in the assassination of Tsar Alexander II on March 13, 1881.

This resulted in the abandonment of that Tsar's plans, to be signed that very day, for a fair measure of liberalization. In the tougher atmosphere of the next few years the terrorist organization was effectively destroyed. There was a last flicker.

Lenin's elder brother, Alexander, was one of the group of students and others who attempted to revive it. They conspired, in amateurish fashion, to assassinate Alexander III. They were discovered, and five of them (including Alexander Ulyanov) were executed on May 20, 1887.

Precisely how this tragedy affected Lenin is difficult to say. Very strongly, without any question. But the story, told much later by one of his sisters, of his remarking, "No, we shall not take that road, our road must be different," is certainly legendary. For, when he first became involved in revolutionary circles at the end of the decade, it was still in the old Narodnik tradition.

He had kept his religious views until 1886, the year of his father's death. Now, aged seventeen, after his brother's execution, he read properly (knowing that it was one of Alexander's favorite books) Chernyskevsky's *What Is to Be Done?* This, Lenin says, "completely transformed my outlook." Under its influence, in 1887–1888, he became a revolutionary, long before he became a Marxist. Chernyshevsky, he later said, not only showed that every right-thinking and really honest man must be a revolutionary, but also showed "what a revolutionary must be like." One thing that Chernyshevsky had written was, "A man with an ardent love of goodness cannot but be a somber monster."

One respect in which, it seems, Lenin's future attitudes may have been affected is in his life-long detestation of liberals. Liberal circles in the town more or less ostracized the Ulyanovs, and their cowardice is said to have made a lasting impression on young Vladimir.

(Ironically enough, one of the exceptions was his head-master, Fyodor Kerensky, father of his later rival, who did everything he could for the young outcast.) In any case, one often gets the impression that in his later life he was to loathe the liberal bourgeois more as a liberal than as a bourgeois.

He was, all the same, admitted to Kazan University later in 1887. After a few months he was one of forty-five students expelled as the result of a demonstration, though his role seems to have been very minor, with his family connections telling against him. It was now that he returned to his mother's estate. In spite of his father's death, the family was comfortably off. He read and studied and was allowed to take his law examinations in 1891.

In 1891–1892 there was a great famine on the Lower Volga. Men of all types and classes threw themselves into the campaign of relief work, the intelligentsia prominently among them. One of the few exceptions was Lenin, who (admittedly under the influence of a most unpleasant woman revolutionary) refused on the grounds that famine, the natural result of the social order, would tend to revolutionize the masses. He commented, "Psychologically this talk of feeding the starving is nothing but an expression of the saccharine-sweet sentimentality so characteristic of our intelligentsia."

Meanwhile the original Populist wave was ending in disintegration and disappointment. Already, in exile in Switzerland, the first Russian Marxist circles had formed, under Georgi Plekhanov. Lenin seems to have become a Marxist in 1891, adopting these views on the role of the proletariat, as Marx too had done, before he had himself laid eyes on an actual industrial worker. In 1893 he moved to St. Petersburg, where he worked as a lawyer and studied Marxist literature. It was not until the following year, when he first met the future Menshevik leader Julius Martov, that he joined an active Marxist group.

Nikolay Valentinov, a young revolutionary of that time, later a colleague of Lenin, explains the attraction of Marxism to men of their type:

> We seized on Marxism because we were attracted by its sociological and economic optimism, its strong belief, buttressed by facts and figures, that the development of the economy, the development of capitalism (this was why we were so interested in it), by demoralizing and eroding the foundations of the old society, was creating new social forces (including us) which would certainly sweep away the autocratic regime together with all its abominations. With the optimism of youth we had been searching for a formula that offered hope, and we found it in Marxism. We were also attracted by its European nature. Marxism came from Europe. It did not smell and taste of home-grown mould and provincialism, but was new, and fresh and exciting.[3]

The mid-1890s saw the apparent triumph of Marxist ideas among the Russian intelligentsia. As Lenin explained, this was partly due to the impermanent anomaly by which Tsarist censorship allowed a good deal of Marxism to be published—taking the view that it was anti-Populist and therefore directed against the then main enemies of Tsarism.

This orthodox Marxism as it reached the intelligentsia had one disadvantage: it implied, or might seem to imply, that the liberation of Russia could come only from the development of capitalism and the maturing of the proletarian classes. Marx himself had said that forty or fifty years of struggle were necessary before even the Western proletariat would be fit to rule. There are many accounts of how this view was received by meetings of intellectuals and students, as implying that the revolutionary struggle would be indefinitely postponed: they saw, in fact, the whole revolutionary élan of the Russian intelligentsia going to waste. For the moment disillu-

[3] *Encounters with Lenin* by Nikolay Valentinov, p. 23.

sionment with Populism was great: but the spirit of revolutionary sanguineness and elitism that it represented remained. In the next decade it was to receive satisfaction both through the Populist revival in the Social Revolutionary Party and through a fusion of the old attitudes with those of Marxism in the Bolshevik Party.

While a section of the Russian revolutionaries led by Plekhanov were becoming orthodox Marxists in the 1880s, Marx had unfortunately come around to the view that the Populists were right. Basing himself on a misunderstanding of the "*Mir*" (village commune) system in Russia, he thought that the country could, after all, come to socialism without the normal capitalist development. He had written to Vera Zasulich that he was now convinced that the rural commune, on which the Populists placed their hopes, could be made "the basis of Russia's social regeneration," and he urged the elimination of the deleterious influences under whose assault it was then coming. That is, he decided against his own Russian disciples. For all Russian Marxists took it that there was no alternative to the development of capitalism in Russia, and that only that path led to socialism.

Russian Marxists were therefore particularly concerned to show that, in the interim since Marx had written, capitalism had after all fully and irretrievably established itself in Russia. This had the advantage that it could then be said (as it was henceforth) that while Marx had hoped that the capitalist road could be avoided, this was unfortunately no longer possible. And in fact, the extraordinary development of industrialization in Russia over the period made the argument thoroughly plausible. Lenin's was the most solid contribution, with his weightiest and best-written book, *The Development of Capitalism in Russia*, the culmination of much polemic and research, which finally came out (quite legally) in 1899.

Over this whole period, 1893–1900, Lenin's Marxism

was "orthodox," and differed little from that of other Russian—and foreign—socialists. There were divergences of opinion on, for example, the stage which Russia had reached. But they all took the classical Marxist view that the proletariat becomes revolutionary by the very nature of its position in society; that the role of the socialist intellectual is the temporary one of not indoctrinating it but helping it clarify and make conscious its own inchoate ideas; and that this teaching and advising did not justify a claim to political leadership. At this time Lenin was writing:

> The task of the party does not consist in thinking up out of its head any kind of modern methods of helping the workers, but in linking itself with the labour movement. . . . The workers acquire an understanding of all this [class consciousness] by constantly drawing it from the very struggle which they are beginning to wage against the factory owners. . . . The struggle of the workers against the factory owners for their daily needs of itself and inevitably forces the workers to think about state, about political questions.

In 1895, after an attack of pneumonia, Lenin got permission to go abroad for his health. In Geneva he had long conversations with Plekhanov, Paul Axelrod, and Vera Zasulich, who had been there, working as Russia's first Marxist center (the Emancipation of Labour group), since 1883. He found them too inclined to forget that collaboration with "liberals" was simply a tactic, not a matter of principle. But on the whole, agreement was general. He undertook effectively to extend the organization into Russia.

On his return, after four months abroad, he broadened his contacts, prepared an illegal newspaper, and joined with young Julius Martov and others in founding the Petersburg League of Struggle for the Emancipation of the Working Class. In December 1895 he was arrested with most of the other members and sent first to prison and then into administrative "free exile" in Siberia.

It was here that he read of, and reacted to, events which were to bring an end to his more or less gradualist and orthodox phase of Marxism and lead to the Leninist version proper.

The Mature Lenin

11

Before we look at the ideas that were to con-
stitute the essentials of "Leninism," it seems
appropriate first to consider the personal and
political character of the thirty-year-old revolutionary who was now reaching his maturity. For
it was, as we have suggested earlier, above all
his personality, specific and individual, which
was to determine the course of events. Others
were to hold the same views, but none were to
have more than a mere fraction of the same
effect.

Marx had argued that
now a portion of the bourgeoisie goes over to
the proletariat, and, in particular, a portion of
the bourgeois ideologists, who have raised
themselves to the level of comprehending
theoretically the historical movement as a
whole.

But what section of the bourgeois intelligentsia? And with what qualities or characteristics?

Marxism's answer, that they are simply those who have accepted Marxist theory, is little more than tautologous. It can hardly be argued that they are just the most intelligent. It is scarcely plausible that they are those who are so lacking in personal passions that objectivity is accepted by them even against their class interests.

The criterion, in fact, is clearly a non-Marxist one, a psychological one. And the Leninist attitude, the Lenin tone, is distinguished from those of other political groups in Russia and elsewhere far less on intellectual grounds than on temperamental ones. It is Lenin's personality, in fact—not simply his powers of intellect and will, but his whole character—which is the center and inspiration of bolshevism, and to an important degree of communism as it still is today.

Lenin was temperamentally suited to a political philosophy of the Marxist type, with its stress on conflict as the motive force of all change. Indeed, it is fair to say that he sharpened and emphasized this aspect of Marxism beyond what seemed appropriate to most Marxists. As he himself put it, the main question in every political and social context was *"Kto-kogo"*—"Who-whom?": that is to say, every situation is essentially a fight which someone wins and someone loses.

He did not strike his followers so much as a cleverer or better or more admirable man than his rivals, but rather as one of much greater force, energy, and determination. Trotsky was to call Lenin "the most highly charged utilitarian who ever came out of history." His main characteristics, in fact, were, first, this complete dedication to his ideas, the total subordination of his personal life, and willingness to sacrifice anything or anybody; second, a lack of personal vanity or ambition combined with an unwavering conviction that on any matter in dispute he alone had the right answer; and third, when (and only when) politics was not in question, occasional kindness to individuals and toleration of oddities.

The concentration and will power were the central features. A prominent young revolutionary colleague of the period, A. N. Potresov, remarked of Lenin many years later,

> No one could sweep people away so much by his plans, impress them by his strength of will, and then win them over by his personality as this man, who at first sight seemed so unprepossessing and crude, and, on the face of it, had none of the things that make for personal charm. Neither Plekhanov, nor Martov, nor anyone else had the secret of that hypnotic influence on or rather ascendancy over people which Lenin radiated. Only Lenin was followed unquestioningly as the indisputable leader, as it was only Lenin who was that rare phenomenon, particularly in Russia—a man of iron will and indomitable energy, capable of instilling fanatical faith in the movement and the cause, and possessed of equal faith in himself. Once upon a time I, too, was impressed by this will power of Lenin's which seemed to make him into a "chosen leader."

This effect was so powerful, the men closest to him were so much under his influence, that, for example (as Trotsky tells us), Grigori Zinoviev and Lev Kamenev even acquired Lenin's handwriting.

His constant principle was not so much his own infallibility (since he several times admitted error after the event) as the correctness of his view at the time, and his right to enforce it at all costs. A member of his own Council of People's Commissars after the Revolution, A. V. Lunacharsky, wrote of him in 1919 that he imposed his will "not because power is sweet to him, but because he is certain that he is right and cannot tolerate anyone spoiling his work." Lunacharsky added that "Lenin's love of power stems from his immense certainty about the rightness of his principles and, probably, from his inability (very useful in a political leader) to put himself in the position of an opponent." This confidence in his own judgment led him several times to remarks such as "The dictatorship of revolutionary classes has often been expressed, supported, and carried out by the dictatorship of individual persons."

Lenin's concentration on political and social revolution was complete. He was unlike the "progressive" type who holds advanced opinions in every field. E. J. Hobsbawm has pointed out[1] that nineteenth-century progressives "pursued natural philosophy, phrenology, free thought, spiritualism, temperance, unorthodox medicine, social reform and the transformation of the family" with more or less equal conviction. *Mutatis mutandis*, a similar package deal—part rational, part fashionable, part crackpot—could be produced for 1917 (or for now). There is none of this in Lenin.

He was, for example, wholly contemptuous of the typical Bolshevik doctor liable to the latest cranky theories of medicine, and advised Gorki in 1912 to avoid them at all costs and go to bourgeois specialists: "Really in ninety-nine cases out of a hundred, doctor-comrades are asses. . . . To try on yourself the discoveries of a Bolshevik—that's terrifying!"

His taste in literature and the arts was equally conventional. He read and admired the usual Russian writers, apart from Dostoevski, though even Tolstoi he praised mainly for his pictures of rural poverty, while saying that he "cannot be forgiven for his views." The writers he particularly liked were the bitter Nekrasov and the satirical Shchedrin, natural choices; Turgenev; and, more interestingly, Chekhov. Of foreign writers, Goethe (in part) and Heine were the only ones with which he was really familiar, among the classics.

He went occasionally to the theater, and was once seen in tears over *La Dame aux Camélias*. In 1919 he

[1] *New Statesman*, April 4, 1969.

opposed a proposal to close down the theaters on the grounds that they were needed, not so much for propaganda as for "the relaxation of employees." On the other hand, in 1922 he was very angry at a decision of the Council of People's Commissars to preserve the Bolshoi Ballet and Opera, denouncing it as "quite indecent" and saying that the money should go into reading rooms. He is quoted, too, as remarking at that time,

> In general, as you probably know, I do not have much sympathy for the intelligentsia, and our slogan "liquidate illiteracy" is in no way to be interpreted as being aimed at the creation of a new intelligentsia. The purpose of "liquidate illiteracy" is only that every peasant should be able to read by himself, without help, our decrees, orders, and proclamations. The aim is completely practical. No more.

Lenin's attitude to the newer styles was extremely hostile—more so, even, than is sometimes reported. On a famous occasion in February 1919, when an actress recited one of Mayakovsky's poems to him, we are told in her memoirs merely that he said that he preferred Pushkin. But the Old Bolshevik V. L. Bonch-Bruyevich, to whom he exploded after the concert, has him using such words as "rubbish" and "shameful." He later referred to "buffoons playing at revolution," and when Lunacharsky, who sympathized with the "New Arts," published Mayakovsky's *150 Million* in five thousand copies, Lenin wrote, "It is rubbish, it is ridiculous, out-and-out ridiculousness and pretentiousness. . . . Lunacharsky should be flogged for his futurism." On another occasion, Lenin was asked what he thought of a "statue" of Prince Kropotkin. He commented merely that he had personally known Kropotkin and the fact was that he really had two eyes and a mouth.

His sexual views were likewise "unprogressive." He disapproved strongly of the attitude of the aristocratic Bolshevik Alexandra Kollontay, who favored what

was then known as free love and spoke of sexual relations in the same terms as taking a glass of water when
one is thirsty. Lenin put it that, even if thirsty, he
preferred not to drink from a glass with the marks of
many lips on it. In fact, the majority of old Bolsheviks
took his view and (like, indeed, the intelligentsia as a
whole) went in for long-term companionships often,
but not always, amounting to official marriage. But here,
as in the question of his literary feelings, he saw no
dispute so essential to the Revolution that he had any
need actually to impose his own views.

Nor should we project on him other sentiments we
might suspect to be inseparable from left-wing opinion.
For example, when in exile he used to go shooting a
good deal. There is a story of his once letting a fox go
because it looked so beautiful: but his main complaint
was that he was a bad shot—unlike Trotsky, who was a
real devotee of the sport. (Engels, it will be remem-
bered, rode to hounds in Cheshire; Marx seems to have
disapproved, though on social rather than humanitarian
grounds.)

As for Lenin's deeper desires: in general, we shall get,
but only very rarely, glimpses of the emotional pressures
held in check by his will power—notably in his extraordinary reaction to the quarrel with Plekhanov (see p.
29). More commonly we find only those emotions
appropriate to the revolutionary struggle—anger, hatred,
impatience, contempt.

In his writings there is a certain lack of precision and
of life when he treats of the promised Communist
future, as in *State and Revolution*. There is a little more
color in some of his remarks about the sufferings of the
poor under capitalism. But real force and vividness, on
the whole, are to be found only in his writings on revolution, and in his polemics against heresy.

His love for humanity in principle is a rarely and
inadequately expressed emotion. The most striking

example is the well-known passage in Gorki's memoirs which quotes Lenin on Beethoven's *Appassionata*:

"Astonishing, superhuman music . . . what miracles people can do. . . . But I can't listen often to music, it affects my nerves, makes me want to say kind stupidities and pat the heads of people who, living in this dirty hell, can create such beauty. But now one must not pat anyone's little head—they would bite off your hand, and one has to beat their little heads, beat mercilessly, although ideally we're against any sort of force against people. Hmm—it's a devilishly difficult task."

But Gorki also noted that Lenin "Has no pity for the mass of the people," and that "the working classes are to Lenin what minerals are to the metallurgist."

Bertrand Russell recorded an even more unfavorable impression: "When I met Lenin, I had much less impression of a great man than I had expected; my most vivid impressions were of bigotry and Mongolian cruelty. . . ." and again, "His guffaw at the thought of those massacred made my blood run cold."[2]

As for his personal feelings, Lenin was always kind and thoughtful to Nadezhda Krupskaya, his wife and companion, support and amanuensis, though there is little sign of anything stronger. Apart from this, it seems clear that he had, in some sense, a certain *tendresse* for Inessa Armand. (It is an inescapable fact that Lenin addressed her as "thou," alone among his women friends.) But there is no evidence that they were lovers in the usual sense. Nor, except in revealing a rare touch of sentiment in a character which might otherwise appear little more than a sort of animated political machine, does the story have much importance. Its main

[2] Bertrand Russell, *Bolshevism: Practice and Theory* (London, 1920), pp. 35–44; *Unpopular Essays* (New York, 1950), p. 171.

interest today is the fact that it is the one episode in Lenin's life any reference to which rouses the present Soviet authorities to the greatest fury—far more than political or intellectual attacks on him.

Though we can note these sentimental, and even emotional, sides of Lenin's personal feelings, how little they amount to in the context of the intensely powerful focusing of all his drives, but for an insignificant penumbra, upon his major concern. Virtually the total force of his personality was concentrated on the broadly political—to a far greater degree than Marx's had been. Everything else in his life appears as no more than mild, brief, and absent-minded relaxation. When some truly nonpolitical matter really took his time and energy, he gave it up, as with chess. The only period after he entered political life when letters and reminiscences have a certain restful, almost idyllic character is the time of his exile in Siberia in 1897–1900. Even that was only comparative: by most standards it was a period of hard work and political activity. From the time of his release in January 1900, his life and character appear as not just predominantly but almost totally political.

What Is to Be Done?

111

In Lenin's absence in exile, the Russian working-class movement had moved in what was for
him a disturbing direction. In the early 1890s it
had been small—a few workers in contact with,
and influenced by, the revolutionary intellectuals
of the Social Democratic groups. With the beginnings of a much larger-scale industrialization,
the workers themselves developed their own local
movements and aims. As in the more advanced
countries, these genuine proletarian leaders and
groups were concerned with trade-union organization and with the immediate struggle over
working conditions, mainly through strikes, and
cared only a little for theory. The larger section
of the Russian Marxists accepted these developments as natural to a maturing proletariat, and
saw their role as one not so much of leading the
new forces but of cooperating with them and
educating them. The immediate duty of Social

Democrats, these "Economists" argued, was to support the workers in their union activity, and so to draw them in the long run into the political fight against Tsarism in alliance with the other opposition parties and classes.

It is clear that Lenin now experienced the same sort of disillusionment about the working class that the People's Will had felt as a result of their "going to" the peasantry in the 1870s. Like them, in a different way, he was driven to a more elitist view of political action.

But it was not only in the Russian labor movement that things were going wrong. While still in exile Lenin read the newly published *Evolutionary Socialism*, by Eduard Bernstein, the first "revisionist." This work, already the focus of violent controversy in the European Social Democratic movement, tended, in a sense, in the same direction as that of the Economists. But Bernstein's was no mere "misapplication" of the Marxist scheme. It was an assertion that Marx had, in certain respects, made a faulty analysis of the whole course of events in the West. Bernstein saw that the rate of profit had not fallen; that wages had not gone down; that there was no sign of the predicted capitalist failure to expand production; that revolutionary situations had not arisen. He concluded that Marx was in error about the inevitable economic dead-end of capitalism, and that it now appeared that wealth could gradually become more diffused and a peaceful transition to socialism be achieved.

Though Bernstein was making explicit the real tendency of the German Social Democrats, that Party's leaders would not give up their old formulas. He was attacked by Karl Kautsky and August Bebel, and his views were voted down by the Party convention. In Russia the old and new revolutionary Marxists united against him, and against the Economists: Plekhanov, Axelrod, Zasulich, together with the young men Lenin, Martov, Potresov.

Soon after his release in 1900, Lenin arrived in

Geneva. Henceforth, except for the two years from November 1905 to December 1907, he was to remain in exile up to the 1917 Revolution. For the man who wished to lead, this was the right choice. The ranking figures of the Russian Social Democrats were all there. Moreover, as Lenin saw, a truly centralized party could be created only from abroad. When it came to the point, it was much easier for an émigré leadership, with the organizational threads and control of the party organs in its hands, to see that the scattered groups and committees in Russia sent the right men abroad to the congresses. It was in exile that the decisive intra-Party struggles would be fought.

To defeat the Economists and create the new revolutionary party which he saw as necessary, the chosen instrument was the new illegal paper, *Iskra* (*The Spark*). It was during a discussion of the editorial statement for the first issue that Lenin had a major quarrel with Plekhanov (over the latter's objection to the clumsy and pedestrian style of Lenin's draft), which gives us one of our few direct insights into Lenin's deeper sentiments.

The same week Plekhanov, by taking a casting vote in the six members of *Iskra*'s editorial board, effectively took it over. Lenin, who was to take over committees and boards by the dozen in similar and often a good deal rougher ways, was totally disenchanted:

We sat there [he and Potresov] . . . we realised we had been made fools of. . . . My "infatuation" with Plekhanov disappeared as if by magic. . . . Never, never in my life have I regarded any other man with such sincere respect and veneration. I have never stood before any man with such "humility" as I stood before him, and never before have I been so brutally spurned. . . . Up to that moment both of us had been enamoured of Plekhanov, and, as we do with our beloved, we forgave him everything, closed our eyes to his shortcomings. . . . Our indignation knew no bounds. . . . Had we not been in love with him, our

conduct would have been different. . . . Young comrades "court" an old comrade out of the great love
they bear him. . . . An enamoured youth receives from
the object of his love a bitter lesson: to regard all
persons "without sentiment"; to keep a stone in one's
sling.

When we think of Lenin as a hard, pragmatic, calcu-
lating man, this quarrel, with its talk of boundless love,
humiliation, disillusionment, will remind us of the
extent to which he shared the emotionalism of the Russian intelligentsia, even though he was henceforth to
keep it under rigid control. It would be hard to parallel
this scene, or rather Lenin's reaction to it, in the history
of any other socialist movement. And the issue was not
even a doctrinal one, but simply whether the young
candidate for the leadership would be in a position to
override his seniors.

Though he talked of giving up the whole project and
returning to Russia, Lenin finally effected a formal truce
with Plekhanov. But even after this breach, and in spite
of a wide variety of political sins later committed by the
older man, Lenin continued to admire him as a theoretician, and some of his work (alone among that of non-
Leninists) is still admitted to the Soviet canon. (The
general orthodoxy of Plekhanov's Marxism was not in
doubt. For example, he argued against the Narodniks
that in their view it would be possible for "Egypt, Persia,
and China to become socialist before the advanced
countries of the West," a formulation accepted by all
the Russian Marxists as showing the self-evident error
of Narodnik ways.)

Meanwhile, Lenin had control of the practical and
organizational side of *Iskra*'s development. While his
colleagues regarded the paper largely as a bearer of
propaganda and agitation and to a lesser extent as a
mutual information bulletin for Social Democrats, for
Lenin it was something quite different. Its role was
twofold. First, it was to propagate among Social Demo-

crats and others his ideas of a tight centralized party; second, the men who smuggled it into Russia and the organizers of circles for reading it were already, by this activity, a reasonably disciplined and centralized organization. Thus Lenin for the first time came into control of a grouping based on himself in Switzerland and radiating outward into Russia. Despite the later vagaries of the *Iskra* board, he retained control of this network. It was a successful start.

In the meantime the fight against Revisionism and Economism was the immediate crux. And in it we see a startling change from the Lenin of *The Development of Capitalism in Russia*. Alasdair MacIntyre, while suggesting that Lenin's swing against the Economists, whose views he had previously more or less shared, was due largely to his reading of Bernstein, feels that this was not so much because he felt Bernstein to be wrong as because he feared that he might be right. The "domestication" of the working classes, partly through the trade unions, might indeed render abortive the revolution foreseen by Marx. But, unlike Bernstein, Lenin concluded that positive subjective action should be taken to prevent this social tendency. The facts adduced by the revisionists were not to be burked. (Leninist explanations of how they could be possible were, however, postponed until 1916, when Lenin finally got around to providing a formal answer in his *Imperialism, the Highest Stage of Capitalism*.) Meanwhile, there were more immediate conclusions.

In the first number of *Iskra*, Lenin had a short article, "Urgent Tasks of Our Movement." It contained two main ideas: first, that the labor movement, unless guided by a "socialist vanguard," would "become petty and inevitably bourgeois," and second, that the vanguard should consist of full-time professionals "who shall devote to the revolution not only their spare evenings but the whole of their lives." This article was incorporated in the famous essay *What Is to Be Done?*, started in 1901 and printed in 1902, which constitutes the central document of Leninism. There the theme is spelled out still more clearly:

> The working class exclusively by its own efforts is able to develop only trade-union consciousness. . . . Modern socialist consciousness can only be brought to them from without . . . can arise only on the basis of profound scientific knowledge. The bearers of science are not the proletariat but the bourgeois intelligentsia. It is out of the heads of members of this stratum that modern socialism originated. . . . Pure and simple trade unionism means the ideological subordination of the workers to the bourgeoisie. . . . Our task is to bring the labour movement under the wing of revolutionary Social Democracy.

Indeed, as he was to sum it up: "Aside from the influence of the Social Democracy, there is no conscious activity of the workers."

We have here, explicit or adumbrated, all the essentials of what was later to be known as Leninism. The view taken in his earlier works, such as the passage quoted on p. 17 from his opinions of the mid-nineties, is now abandoned—indeed, contradicted. The earlier strain of elite revolutionism which Lenin had learned from Chernyshevsky and the rest, and the idea of mass social movements derived from Marx which had temporarily seemed to supersede the other, were now brought together. And it is worth nothing that "Bolsheviks" and "Mensheviks" alike shared at least the view of the conscious party bringing leadership to the masses from outside, though they were to disagree on the organization of that party: in both, the famous dictum of Marx and Engels, "The emancipation of the working class is the task of the working class itself," received decisive amendment.

Lenin derives most of his doctrinal and textual support from the early Marx—that is, not the now fashionable pre-Marxist Marx, but the Marx of the Communist

League period. But those early organizational principles were, of course, those of small, semiconspiratorial groups which preceded the rise of large-scale working-class movements and were superseded by them. As nuclei for developing Marxist ideas and bringing them to the attention of the incipient proletariats, they were defensible in terms of classical Marxism for the early phase, but not for any later period.

That early Marxism had been the Marxism of a largely autocratic Europe, and as the autocracies fell or became milder it ceased to be applied in the West. The new "Leninism," in fact, was a primitive Marxism in two senses. It was the Marxism of the early Marx, and it was the Marxism of a backward Europe. The later Marx, and the maturer working classes, had progressed or become corrupted, depending on how one looks at it.

Lenin had already shown a good deal of virulence in polemics against first the Populists and then the "Legal Marxists" (like Peter Struve, who, after prominence in the Social Democratic "First Congress" in 1898—itself illegal—evolved into liberalism). But the attack on the Economists, as well as being the first statement of his own particular views, was his first major battle honor actually as a leader in the intra-Party struggle. In it his organizational and controversial techniques were clearly exhibited.

For very few of the Economists, in fact, held the view Lenin attributed to them. They fully supported the idea of the Social Democrats' taking their conceptions to the working class. The way they looked at it was, in fact, that through the collaboration of Social Democrats in trade-union and other developments, the working class would come to accept their ideas and their guidance as better-informed comrades by natural discussion rather than sectarian harangue.

The first important example of Lenin's controversial methods was to mark the whole period. He often repeated with approval a remark of Plekhanov's: "First, let's stick the convict's badge on him, and after that we can examine his case." So it was, right through the period, as when he quite falsely called the Mensheviks of the later part of the decade "liquidators," alleging that they wished to dissolve the Party organization. At the same time, in all these cases, he was a great proponent of the method of implying guilt by association. If any of those he was attacking held a given view, it was attributed equally to all the others. But, as Lenin himself put it (when arraigned before a Party court in 1907 for the tenor of his attacks on the Mensheviks), his controversial methods were

> calculated to evoke in the reader hatred, aversion and contempt . . . calculated not to convince but to break up the ranks of the opponent, not to correct the mistake of the opponent but to destroy him, to wipe his organization off the face of the earth. This formulation is indeed of such a nature as to evoke the worst thoughts, the worst suspicions about the opponent. . . .[1]

The striking point here is not so much Lenin's tactics in controversy—though these were of such a nature as to revolt even many of his sympathizers—as his open statement of them. Political and other controversy is often conducted to some extent through unfair imputation and irrelevant smear. But it is seldom that this is entirely conscious and explicit. Lenin's logic here is that of his whole moral attitude. Marx had doubtless tended to a pragmatic and relativist view of morality, but he had also spoken of "the simple laws of ethics and justice by which individuals must be guided in mutual relationships, and which must be the supreme laws of conduct between States." Lenin's formulation is strikingly different: "Our morality is completely subordinated to the interests of the class struggle of the proletariat. . . .

[1] Lenin, *Selected Works*, English edition, III, 486.

Morality is that which serves to destroy the old exploiting society." Therefore, "We deny all morality that is drawn from some conception beyond men, beyond class. We say that it is a deception . . . a fraud and a stultification of the minds of the workers and peasants in the interests of the landowners and capitalists."

This was to remain a basic principle of the Leninist style of controversy. After the Revolution, for example, the Italian left-wing socialist leader Serrati, though generally sympathetic to the Communists, tried to prevent Lenin from splitting his movement. Lenin attacked him in terms which struck the then Secretary of the Comintern , Angelica Balabanoff, as both gross and dishonest. Zinoviev was sent to explain things to her: "We have fought and slandered him because of his great merits. It would not have been possible to alienate the masses [from him] without resorting to these means."

Lenin was prepared to use any means whatever to forward the struggle (as he put it, "Everything that is done in the proletarian cause is honest"). Still, while he used and justified abuse, smears, falsifications of his opponents' arguments, and so on, he never turned to the more superficial tinsel of leadership. Stalin recounts how, when he first met him at the Tammerfors Conference he felt it out of place that a leader did not hold himself aloof and make a ceremonious entry, but simply mingled modestly with the other delegates. That sort of meretriciousness was wholly alien to Lenin's character.

Over the next seventeen years, Lenin was to have a series of bitter disputes with other Russian Marxists. With one exception, they were not about Marxist doctrine at all, since his opponents almost invariably held views quite as orthodox as his own on all the political and social teachings of Marx and Engels. They were on issues of party organization or of immediate political tactics, or (as a product of these) were disputes that arose between Lenin and disciples orthodox on the particular controversy but wishing to compromise in one way or another with the heretics in question.

Not until we come to the time of *Imperialism* do we find a theoretical dispute—and not with anyone in Russia so much as with Karl Kautsky. Nor, even here, was the matter one of Marxist orthodoxy or principle, since Marx had not dealt with the subject at all.

Faction and Revolution

•

IV

In 1903 the "Second" Social Democratic Party Congress met in Brussels and later in London. Its original purpose, from Lenin's point of view, was to crush the Economists. This was done easily since, as Lenin himself explained, "the composition of the Party Congress was settled in advance by the Organization Committee." The Economists had a majority among the Social Democrats in St. Petersburg and were supported by a large part of the emigration: but they were allowed only 3 voting delegates out of 51. There were a number of other delegates from non-Iskraite groups, but the solid Iskraite vote of 33 was a clear organizational victory.

But, as ever, a new split occurred among the victors. For Lenin now took the decision to press even further his insistence on an elite party. He had already written, in *What Is to Be Done?*, "The organisations of revolutionists must be composed first and foremost of people whose profession is that of revolutionist. . . . As this is the common feature of the members of such an organisation, all distinctions as between workers and intellectuals must be dropped." And, in fact, he was to insist that worker revolutionaries should be withdrawn from actual factory work, to become full-time party operatives, living on party funds.

On the eve of the Congress, Lenin had put the organizational point clearly in a letter to Plekhanov, urging "as much centralisation as possible. Autonomy of local committees in local matters, with the right of veto by the Central Committee. . . . District organisation only with the agreement and approval (of its personnel) by the Central Committee." Lenin's advocacy of the tightly disciplined organization was based in part on the idea that repression made conspiratorial tactics necessary and in part on the backwardness of the Russion working class, but was also intended to counter the inefficiency and woolly-mindedness of the Russian intelligentsia. It seemed clear that the bulk of the Iskraites had not fully understood the implications of *What Is to Be Done?*

In the Congress discussion on the Party program Martov put forward a definition of a Party member: "one who recognizes the Party's program and supports it by material means and by regular personal assistance under the direction of one of the Party organizations." Lenin insisted on "one who recognizes the Party's program and supports it by material means and by personal participation in one of the Party's organizations."

The difference does not look enormous (especially in Russian underground conditions), nor did Lenin himself take the mere phrasing too formally. He had noted in the earlier debates a certain "softness" among many Iskraite delegates, and chose this issue as his means of dividing "soft" from "hard": "My formula restricts the conception of Party worker while Martov's broadens it."

Martov saw the real issue too: he urged a broad party, not restricted to professional revolutionaries.

Lenin was defeated by 28 votes to 22. Plekhanov supported him, but all the other leading Iskraites voted against him. Even the extreme young revolutionist Trotsky joined them, saying that, while it was wrong for the Party to follow behind the working class and its economic demands, the Leninist view, by which the Party separated itself from the working class and "undertook its obligations," was equally false to Marxism. Lenin won a single important vote, after various delegates had left: by 22 votes to 20 with two abstentions, he and Plekhanov established control of *Iskra*. This was the famous "majority-minority" whose names were henceforward applied to Lenin's "Bolsheviks" and Martov's "Mensheviks," respectively—a clever, preemptive propagandist move by the Leninists.

By now, Lenin's ideas give all the essentials, if not yet the formal thesis, of "democratic centralism," which later became (and remains) the official organizational principle of the Communist parties. The "centralism," in fact, came first, and was the essential, and the "democratic" was dependent on the centralism, since the center could in fact dictate the composition of the representation of the localities. It will be appropriate here, if only to show the permanence of this main theme, to quote two documents of a later date, when the whole position had been elaborated. The first is a resolution of the Eighth Party Congress in 1919 drafted by Lenin:

> The party is in a position in which the strictest centralism and the most stringent discipline are absolute necessities. All decisions of higher headquarters are absolutely binding for the lower. Every decision must first of all be executed, and only after that an appeal to the corresponding party organ is permissible. In this sense, outright military discipline is indispensable in the party at the present time.

The second is from his application of this principle on an international scale, in a Resolution of the Second Congress of the Comintern in 1921:

> The main principle of democratic centralism is that of the higher cell being elected by the lower cell, the absolute binding force of all directives of a higher cell for a cell subordinate to it, and the existence of a commanding party centre [whose authority is] indisputable for all leaders in party life, from one congress to the next.

All those revolutionaries who criticized Lenin's views of Party organization, from Martov to Trotsky and the great Polish revolutionary Rosa Luxemburg, argued that "democratic centralism" would lead to autocracy. Though Lenin was prepared to argue this was not the case, he also made it clear that he did not mind even if it was. He had to rebuke Nikolai Bukharin in 1921 for his "failure to understand that formal democracy must be subordinated to revolutionary expediency." In March 1918 he asserted, "There is absolutely no contradiction in principle between Soviet democratism and the use of dictatorial power by single individuals. . . . How can the strictest unity of will be ensured? By the subordination of the will of thousands to the will of one." And in 1920 he went as far as to say, "The will of the class is sometimes given effect by a dictator, who sometimes does more alone, and often is more necessary."

As Rosa Luxemburg now pointed out (finding it suitable as early as 1904 to call her essay "Leninism or Marxism?"), the view was "ultra-centralist." It consisted of, as she put it,

> on the one hand, the sharp separation of the organized bodies of outspoken and active revolutionists from the unorganized though revolutionary active masses surrounding them, and on the other hand, strict discipline and direct, decisive and determining intervention of the central authorities in all expressions of life in the party's local organizations. It suffices to

note, for example, that the central committee, according to this conception, is authorized to organize all subcommittees of the party, hence also has the power to determine the personal composition of every single local organization, from Geneva and Liège to Tomsk and Irkutsk, to give it a set of self-made local statutes, to completely dissolve it by a decree and create it anew, and finally [and this was to be the key point] in this manner to influence the composition of the highest party authority, the Party Congress. According to this, the central committee appears as the real active nucleus of the party, and all other organizations merely as its executive organs.

She was able to show, moreover, that great mass movements of the proletariat had in fact taken place in Russia, and that these more or less spontaneous surges had almost nothing to do with the Bolshevik organization—while their mere existence effectively refuted the Leninist claim: "Nothing will more surely enslave a young labor movement to an intellectual elite hungry for power than this bureaucratic straitjacket, which will immobilize the movement and turn it into an automaton manipulated by a Central Committee."

The old Marxist Axelrod took the view that if the workers were subordinated in this way to the revolutionary intelligentsia they might be used in the ensuing revolution as mere cannon fodder, as they had been by other classes in earlier revolutions. Trotsky's comment was the celebrated and prophetic remark that "the organization of the Party takes the place of the Party itself; the Central Committee takes the place of the organization; and finally the dictator takes the place of the Central Committee."

But in fact, the revulsion against Lenin seems to have been at least as much a matter of dislike of his actual conduct of the struggle as of his principles. He himself had not actually planned a split, and was for some time rather at a loss as to whether to go ahead after so much resistance. His *Collected Works* for the period is full of letters of compromise (and of ultimata, drafted but not sent). Pleased though he was to draw the lines, he was surprised and sorry that so many delegates had interpreted his formulation as a blueprint for absolute Lenin leadership. It seems clear that he had forfeited much support actually during the Congress by his intransigent tactics. The opposition of Martov and others, that is, was far less an abstract matter than one of distrust at what seemed to them a claim to authoritarian infallibility.

The breach with Martov, in particular, was a personal blow to Lenin: they had been colleagues in their first young revolutionary actions. For ever after, Lenin (his wife tells us) was always to welcome signs of grace, from his point of view, in Martov's stands. He had lost his affection, but not his respect, for Plekhanov; he now lost his respect, but not his affection, for Martov.

The Social Democrats remained, in theory, a single party. Until 1912, the struggles were for the Party vote, the Party purse, the Party mind. Lenin threw himself into the factional strife. As he wrote later, he "conducted himself like a madman" at the meeting of the Iskraite faction that followed the Congress. His new young Leninists gave him a majority of 9 to 7. He then held a meeting at which guards excluded his opponents. He was now hardly sleeping or eating, but spending his entire time in political work; continuous pressure was, for example, put on Trotsky to change sides, though without effect.

Within months after the Second Congress Lenin had lost the fruits of his majority votes. Plekhanov finally refused to go along further with the crushing of his old colleagues. Lenin lost *Iskra*; and the majority he had acquired in the Central Committee, after refusing to back him in an attempt to recapture the paper by force, later also turned against him.

It now became clear that his view of party organization was by no means formalist. When he controlled

Iskra but not the Central Committee, Trotsky had put the view to him that "the central organ [i.e. *Iskra*] should be subordinated to the Central Committee."

"That won't do," Lenin replied. "That is contrary to the relative strength. How can they direct us from Russia? It won't do. . . . We are the stable centre and shall direct from here."

"But doesn't that mean complete dictatorship by the central organ?" Trotsky asked.

"What is there bad about that?" Lenin answered. "In the present situation, it cannot be otherwise."

On losing *Iskra*, Lenin reversed that position. And later, when he lost control of both, he was to defy both and set up his own "Central Committee" with whatever credentials he could scrape up. His consistency lay, as ever, less in any organizational theory than in the conviction that his views must be made to prevail.

For the moment he was left with a small group of supporters, of whom the most prominent was A. A. Bogdanov. Unfortunately Bogdanov was attracted by recent developments in philosophy and took the view that the "empiriomonism" he drew from Ernst Mach and Richard Avenarius could be assimilated to Marxism. Lenin, who had read of, and even skimmed the work of, these two, had instantly concluded that their thought was "idealistic claptrap" and could only mean total ideological degeneration and "revisionism." But when Plekhanov raised the issue against Bogdanov, Lenin felt compelled to say that this was an attempt to divert attention from the real problems of the Party, and he declared a "truce" on the philosophical front— for the time being.

All but two of the Central Committee were arrested in Russia in February 1905, and Lenin seized his opportunity. He had the two survivors summon a "Third Congress," which even he admitted was formally illegal. Even this Congress, however, though almost entirely "Bolshevik," refused to expel or discipline the Mensheviks and other deviants. Lenin's control, in fact, remained shaky. In particular it had little effect in Russia itself.

For since the Social Democratic Party remained, at least formally, a single organization, the factions which competed so fiercely in Switzerland and elsewhere in the emigration had less significance at home. In the big cities, indeed, the faction fight simmered, but even there it was much less fierce than abroad; in fact, it had to be stirred up continually by messengers from émigré headquarters. In more distant parts of Russia, the underground struggle against Tsarism took up so much of the energy of all concerned that there was little left for what were often ill-comprehended doctrinal divisions.

For the country was entering on a great revolutionary crisis. The first revolutionary actions had been a series of assassinations, in particular that of the reactionary minister V.K. Plehve in 1904. For now, just when the Marxists' triumph among the intelligentsia had seemed complete and Populism had looked quite dead, the latter had powerfully re-emerged in the new Social Revolutionary Party. Over the following years (and even in the elections to the Constituent Assembly that followed the October Revolution in 1917) the SRs showed themselves able to win mass support greater than that which went to the Bolsheviks. This was not due to any superior political skill; in general the leadership was mediocre and almost always ready to sacrifice political advantage to considerations of abstract principle. But as soon as the SR party was founded, it began to attract many of Russia's more impatient and energetic young rebels. Reviving the weapon of assassination, it once again offered them immediate action in a way that the Marxists could not. And, as with its predecessors of the 1870s, it put much of its faith in the peasantry. The peasant question, on which Lenin was often to shift his tactical position, now received his serious doctrinal attention.

In 1905 he published *Two Tactics of Social Democracy in the Revolution*, came out. Lenin's theme was that Russia was on the verge of a bourgeois revolution. But the Russian bourgeoisie was so weak, vacillating, and generally incompetent that it was incapable of carrying it out. The proletarian party should therefore enter into a "democratic dictatorship of the proletariat and peasantry" whose task would be that of the bourgeois revolution. After this was completed would come the proletariat's struggle against the petty bourgeois representatives of the peasantry.

The advantage of this formulation was that it provided a way in which the proletarian party could lay its hands on the instruments of power and prepare the ground for further action, even when a country was admittedly not ripe for proletarian revolution proper. Lenin again showed an intuitive grasp of the best way to reconcile Marxist convictions and Russian revolutionary hopes. The Mensheviks saw the forthcoming revolution as inevitably bourgeois, and after it a long period of peaceful organizational work. Trotsky developed his theory of "permanent revolution" by which the post-revolutionary regime would quickly run through the bourgeois revolution into the socialist one. The Mensheviks were too unmilitant for the young Marxist activists, while Trotsky put too much strain on their Marxist categories. But Lenin, taking a stand between these views, gave the party the prospect of entering into and, for the time being at least, gaining a large measure of control over the bourgeois revolution while avoiding the appearance either of opportunism or of adventurism.

As for the prospects of the peasantry in the longer run, "We must," he wrote, "stand firm on our own proletarian class point of view: we must organize the rural proletariat as we do the urban, and combine them in an independent class party. We must explain . . . the hostile clash of their interests with those of the bourgeois peasantry and must call them to battle for the socialist revolution."[1]

This was never to be a sound analysis. The "rural proletariat" was a backward and unreliable stratum, a sort of lumpen-peasantry. The forces in the countryside had been wrongly estimated. The whole future of Communist failure with the peasantry is here.

Meanwhile, revolution had started in St. Petersburg, with the police firing on the mass demonstration led by Father Gapon on Bloody Sunday, January 9, 1905. The revolutionary parties had played virtually no part at all in arousing the masses, and Lenin had to ask, "Can the Social Democrats seize this spontaneous movement?" Both factions together could only claim a following of a few hundred workers as late as March. In Sevastopol, the most violent focus of revolution, though Social Democrats finally played a leading part, there seem to have been no Bolsheviks at all.

In the great cities, "soviets" arose for the first time as central strike, and later insurrectional, committees of the workers. The Bolsheviks played no part in their origins and little in their development. At first, indeed, they refused to take part in a soviet at all if it did not officially accept the Social Democratic program. Lenin himself regarded them as useful organizations, though at first he took the view that in the long run, when Social Democrats' work among the masses was on a truly broad and solid scale, such institutions might become effectively superfluous. But by November, when a general strike and insurrection had come, he condemned the earlier Bolshevik attitude and for the first time urged that the soviet should declare itself the provisional revolutionary government of Russia with representatives of "all the revolutionary parties and all the revolutionary democrats," on a broad minimum program, and pending the calling of a constituent assembly.

[1] *Proletariat and Peasantry*, in *Collected Works*, VII, 158.

There was really no choice: the Bolsheviks could either remain isolated and totally ineffective or merge themselves in the mainstream and hope to make some progress. Moreover, Lenin even felt obliged to relax the whole rigor of the disputes on dogma and tactics. For as the revolutionary wave swept on, the St. Petersburg Soviet, partly as a result of Bolshevik dogmatism, came largely under Menshevik leadership and the great struggles saw Trotsky, in particular, to the fore.

Lenin did not reach Russia until November. In fact, he arrived as a result of the amnesty which formed part of the concessions by whose means the regime took the edge off the revolutionary spirit. In December the government felt strong enough to move against the Soviet leaders and the revolutionary press. A renewed strike wave, with an insurrection in Moscow, resulted. This time the Bolsheviks played an important part. Lenin was not directly involved, but he had been studying and preaching revolutionary tactics since his arrival, going into extraordinary detail in his instructions about killing policemen, and the use of every conceivable weapon, from rifles and bombs to knuckle-dusters and boiling water, in passages to which (as Bertram Wolfe remarks) no parallel could be found in the writings of such practical leaders of insurrection as Trotsky and Rosa Luxemburg.

By the end of the year the government had regained control, and though there were local outbreaks and a large number of SR assassinations in the next couple of years, and though Lenin himself continued to hope for some time that the crisis would break out again, the Revolution was effectively over.

Reaction

The end of the revolutionary phase (though it was not recognized as such, even by Lenin, for some time) faced him and the other revolutionaries with a new situation. The great concession, made on October 30, 1905, had been the granting of a constitution. Over the following years, the condition of complete illegality for all opponents of the regime, which had been the great justification for conspiratorial organizational principles, no longer applied. Not that the new constitutionalism, or the new liberties, were very impressive by Western standards. The franchise, unsatisfactory from the start, was continually narrowed. The First Duma, elected in May 1906, was dissolved after two months, and the second after three. The third and fourth each lasted their full terms, but were heavily weighted against opposition representation.

Nevertheless, this was a fundamental shift

from total repression. Whatever the inequities and difficulties, revolutionaries in the following period were able
to stand for election and be elected. There were to be
eighteen, then five, and later six Bolsheviks in the
Duma. And (though again under difficulties) the opposition—even the Bolsheviks—was able to issue legal
periodicals. The problems, in fact, were new ones.

And in these changed conditions, in the ensuing
period, as the country gradually settled down and the
revolutionary movement shrank and decayed, Lenin was
involved in a number of matters peripheral to the direct
struggle with Tsarism, though (in their different ways)
of great significance to the Bolshevik cause. Faction, the
continuing struggle with fresh deviations, needed, as
ever, constant attention; philosophy for the first time
seemed to require his urgent intervention; and funds to
keep his organization in existence were a pressing and
increasing concern.

By the end of 1905, the new mass membership had
forced the reunification of most of the Bolshevik and
Menshevik groups still split—particularly in St. Petersburg itself. Lenin opposed this. But partly because of
their superior record in the Revolution, the Mensheviks
won an easy majority at the Fourth Party Congress in
Stockholm in April 1906, and here full reunification
was carried through. As the up-and-coming young Bolshevik Zinoviev tells us, "Under the pressure of the
masses, the general staff of the Bolsheviks and Mensheviks were forced to unite. At the Congress victory
was with the Mensheviks . . . there was nothing for the
Bolsheviks but to submit."

But the Menshevik majority took no serious action to
consolidate its power in the Party. The Bolsheviks set
up a "center" which was both secret and, as one of their
annalists remarks, also "as far as the party was concerned, illegal," with a view to preparing insurrection,
for Lenin still believed that a new revolutionary wave
was imminent.

A vitriolic attack on the Mensheviks late in 1906, in which Lenin quite falsely accused them of a conspiracy with the liberal Constitutional Democrats, led the long-suffering Central Committee to set up a "court of honor" to deal with him. But at the London (Fifth) Congress in April–May 1907, he once again gained a small majority on most issues. (The "court" was of course instantly wound up.) The main issue was now participation or otherwise in the Duma.

The elections to the First Duma in the spring of 1906 had been boycotted by the revolutionary parties with Lenin's hesitant approval. Partly as a result of this, the Constitutional Democratic Party, founded in October 1905, had emerged as a powerful new force. The Mensheviks now saw their error and rejected the boycott for the future, and Lenin, too, privately thought it had been a mistake and publicly said that it should henceforth be avoided. But he now found himself faced with a *Left* deviation. At a Party conference in August 1907 the Bolshevik faction voted 14–1 against him on this issue —unanimously, that is, except for himself. They refused to name him their spokesman at the conference, and chose Bogdanov instead. But with the Mensheviks and others, Lenin was able to outvote them.

After the elections, when Social Democratic deputies sat in the Duma, Bogdanov and his friends were continually urging their recall, and became known as Otzovists, or Recallers. Even Lenin's closest associates of the new period, Zinoviev and Kamenev, came out against him. But Lenin's estimate of the situation, it soon became obvious, was the right one. Many of his opponents gradually rejoined him. As the Marxist historian M. Pokrovsky, one of the most original minds in the movement, remarked:

> There was, above all, his enormous capacity to see to the root of things, a capacity which finally awakened in me a sort of superstitious feeling. I frequently had occasion to differ from him on practical questions but

I came off badly every time. When this experience had been repeated about seven times, I ceased to dispute and submitted to Lenin even if logic told me that one should act otherwise. I was henceforth convinced that he understood things better and was master of the power denied to me, of seeing about ten feet down into the earth.[1]

With Bogdanov and his adherents in opposition, Lenin felt free to attack the "Machist" philosophical views of his rival. Already in 1904 he had prepared notes refuting the voluminous and subtle philosophical works of Mach and Avenarius after having in his possession two of their books, 1200 pages in all, for two and a half days. The notes he had then made, but not published in view of the political situation, he now expanded into his *Materialism and Empirio-Criticism*, the only philosophical work he ever had printed in his lifetime, and still an authoritative text in the U.S.S.R.

Materialism and Empirio-Criticism is otherwise seldom taken seriously as a philosophical work (though Korsch has some interesting and not wholly hostile comments). In effect, it is a defense and restatement of Engels' and Plekhanov's interpretation of the Marxist philosophy. The main direction of thrust is to represent Mach and Bogdanov as implying the insubstantiality or unknowability of the material universe. This involves, first, the assertion of the primacy of matter, and of thought as a product of the evolution of matter; second, the existence, apart from sensations, of a material universe (and here Lenin's common sense points out that this does not indicate any special view of the "materiality" of matter, and is not contradicted by recent conceptions of matter in terms of energy states); and third, a presentation of cognition, in a very crude fashion, as being a "reflection" in the human mind of material

[1] Bertram D. Wolfe, *Three Who Made a Revolution* (New York, 1966).

reality. As Dr. George Lichtheim points out in the volume in this series on Georg Lukács, all this is really no more than a restatement of eighteenth-century materialist philosophy.

As for the "dialectical" features, first is the assertion that while earlier materialisms insisted on matter occurring in gross lumps, the dialectic and only the dialectic could admit a more sophisticated view; second comes the idea that cognition involves "interpenetration" between mind and matter, and that "knowing" the universe is a question of the knower's manipulating it; third, and more generally, the dialectic represents the ways in which the processes of the universe take place —in fact, by "contradiction," the "unity of opposites," the "transformation of quantity into quality," and in general the Hegelian-Marxist terminology of struggle and sharp changes.

As a polemic, the book is characterized by Lenin's usual controversial methods. He simply asserted that the positivists were "idealists," and even "solipsists"; and he attributed to Bogdanov anything that had been said by any other Machists, including points on which Bogdanov had specifically disagreed with them. *Materialism and Empirio-Criticism* made little mark at the time. (The cool comments of one of the few who bothered to reply to it, Lyubov Axelrod, are, surprisingly enough, included in editions of Lenin's *Collected Works* that came out in Russia as late as the mid-twenties.)

Later (in the early part of the war) Lenin started to read Hegel seriously. The "Philosophical Notebooks" which he then wrote for his own use are rather more sophisticated, though still hardly impressive. He concluded in the end that Marx—and in particular *Capital* —could not be understood without the knowledge of Hegelian logic, so that for fifty years no Marxist had yet understood him! Lenin seems, in fact, to have come to Hegel as that section of the Holy Writ, or at least its Apocrypha, which he had simply been too busy to read before. While treating much of Hegel as "nonsense," he was yet shifted from the cruder standpoints of his "materialism," at least for the time being, in these private notes. This does not seem to have altered his political attitudes. All the same, his interest in Hegel was genuine enough, and after the Revolution he tried to inculcate the knowledge of Hegelianism—instructing, for example, the editors of the new theoretical magazine *Under the Banner of Marxism* to pay great attention to it. Still, the "notebooks" are hardly to be taken as part of his teaching any more than abandoned drafts can be taken as truly part of a poet's œuvre, however interesting to specialist students.

Nor did Lenin ever reconcile in his mind the "Engelsian" with the "Hegelian" strains of the dialectic. As the result he was able, for example, to make such paradoxical estimates as his characterization of Bukharin (in his "Testament") as "a most valuable and most distinguished party theoretician" and in the same sentence as inadequately Marxist on the ground that "he has never studied and never fully understood dialectics."

These questions of philosophy arose, in fact, peripherally to, and later than, Lenin's central convictions. The importance, such as it is, of *Materialism and Empirio-Criticism* lies largely in the fact that it became the Talmud of Soviet official philosophy, and has since been effectively used to bludgeon deeper, or other, development and analysis.

Even so, this was a comparatively minor matter amid the general regimentation of Party thought in the post-Lenin period. More generally, one's feeling is that in Russia—as in Britain and America—the philosophical "front" was never a very important one, either in Lenin's time or later. The emphasis placed on these problems, and the extent to which they infected and involved the left-wing intellectuals of Central Europe, Italy, and, to a slightly lesser extent, France, must astonish Russian and Anglo-Saxon alike. When George Lichtheim remarks, in passing, that "a generation of students was corrupted" by a philosopher, we may feel that nothing really comparable could have happened in Russia or Britain or the U.S.A.

The breach with Bogdanov and his supporters also led Lenin into a controversy with Maxim Gorki and others on the whole question of religious feeling, however distant from the established faiths. A number of former revolutionaries were turning to philosophies concerned with problems regarded by Marxism as inessential or nonexistent, such as the "meaning of life." Some of them simply adopted mystical views; others—and this Lenin regarded as worse still—attempted to combine such views with Marxism. As with those who had tried to bring Marxism into line with the new empiriocritical philosophies, he fought them fiercely. Considerable insight into his attitudes can be gained by comparing his pronouncements on religion with those of Marx. Marx was by no means lacking in controversial acerbity. But this famous definition of religion as "the opium of the people" is far from carrying the harshness that the bare phrase may imply. It comes in the course of a humane and sensitive passage: "Religion is the sigh of the oppressed creature, the heart of a heartless world, the spirit of soulless stagnation. It is the opium of the people."

Lenin repeated the phrase in a characteristically sharper tone: "Religion is the opium of the people. . . . Religion is a kind of spiritual gin in which the slaves of capital drown their human shape and their claims to any decent life." And going even further, he wrote to Gorki,

> Every religious idea, every idea of God, even flirting with the idea of God, is unutterable vileness . . . vileness of the most dangerous kind, "contagion" of the most abominable kind. Millions of sins, filthy deeds,

acts of violence and physical contagions . . . are far less dangerous than the subtle, spiritual idea of a God decked out in the smartest "ideological" costumes. . . . Every defence or justification of the idea of God, even the most refined, the best intentioned, is a justification of reaction.

But the great intellectual event of the prewar period was the publication in 1909 of the collection *Vekhi*, in which the new generation of liberal intellectuals argued the obsolescence and narrow perspectives of the Russian revolutionary intelligentsia—reflecting, in a sense, the new possibilities, hostile to both revolution and autocracy, which marked the reconstruction associated with the great Tsarist minister of the period, P. A. Stolypin.

For the new moods among the intelligentsia, the abandonment of revolutionary irreconcilability in favor of an evolutionary process in which independent civic and political trends would come to life and turn Russia into a modern state on the Western pattern, were as repulsive to Lenin (b. 1870) as they were to Tsar Nicholas II (b. 1868). A new generation was seeing different perspectives from those of the established faiths. For the time being Nicholas, to some degree chastened by the experience of 1905, was allowing Stolypin to begin the economic, social, and even if only to a very partial degree the political, reconstruction of Russia.

Lenin had the utmost respect for the will and intelligence of Stolypin. He remarked, "Our reactionaries are distinguished by the extreme clarity of their class consciousness. They know very well what they want, where they are going, and on what forces they can count."

He noted the attempt to create a prosperous peasantry:

Economic inevitability unquestionably causes and is effecting the most far-reaching upheaval in Russia's agricultural order. The question is only whether this is to be brought about by the landlords led by the

Tsar and Stolypin, or by the peasant masses led by the proletariat.[2]

And (in 1908) he saw the danger to the whole revolutionary cause:

> The Stolypin Constitution and the Stolypin agrarian policy mark a new phase in the breakdown of the old, semi-patriarchal and semi-feudal system of tsarism, a new movement toward its transformation into a middle-class monarchy. . . . It would be empty and stupid democratic phrase-mongering to say that the success of such a policy in Russia is "impossible." It is possible! If Stolypin's policy is continued . . . then the agrarian structure of Russia will become completely bourgeois.[3]

(And in fact by 1917 the peasants already owned more than three-quarters of the land. The gain in arable land to the peasantry of all the confiscations and reforms of the Revolution was about sixteen per cent.)

Meanwhile, with the general fading-out of the active revolutionary movement, the Duma at least provided a platform for speeches in which the Party line could be made available to the public. In the following years Lenin himself wrote many of the speeches for the Bolshevik deputies. If the idea was not quite as effective as it might have been, it was partly because these speeches were not always suited either to the immediate occasion or to the Russian situation in general; and partly because the Bolshevik deputies were almost without exception distinguished much more for Leninist loyalty than for oratory, quick-wittedness, high political intelligence, or other qualities useful for their positions. As a result, they were largely outshone by the Mensheviks and others.

[2] *Political Remarks, Collected Works,* XII, 125.
[3] *Proletarii* [Bolshevik newspaper], in *Collected Works,* XII, 193.

The one good speaker was Roman Malinovsky, who became head of the Bolshevik faction in the Duma. As one of the few leading Bolsheviks of working-class origin, Malinovsky was particularly admired by Lenin, who defended him even when he had committed errors which would ordinarily have attracted his censure. In particular, when Malinovsky suddenly resigned his position in the Duma and left Russia, Lenin fully accepted his side of the story, and attacked the Mensheviks for having persecuted him till he had a breakdown. The truth is that Malinovsky was an agent of the secret police (Okhrana), and his employers had ordered him to give up the post. He was already under strong suspicion in Party quarters, but Lenin continued to defend him.

Malinovsky was only the most prominent of the many Okhrana agents who penetrated the top levels of the Party. As early as the Second Congress a police agent had penetrated Lenin's entourage: in the faction fights that followed, he sided with Lenin on every occasion. A member of the five-man Bolshevik group in the Third Duma was a police agent. So was one of the two Bolshevik members of the Bureau of Émigré Organizations set up in 1908. In general, the police representatives were under instructions to support, and even to incite, Lenin and his group in the factional struggle—taking the view, quite correctly as far as it went, that the splitting and disorganization of the revolutionary movement in general could best be achieved through him.

But if the Malinovsky question caused argument and censure within the movement, this was nothing compared with the dispute over "expropriations."

Lenin's principle of withdrawing workers from the factories and enrolling them as full-time professional revolutionaries, in fact his whole conception of a large professional organization, carried one important problem: professionals have to be paid. The question of the income of the Bolsheviks up to 1917 is a complicated one involving a number of moral and political issues. It is also a very obscure one, and to this day there are early sources of income, known only under code names, which have not yet been wholly explained.

Much of the revolutionaries' money came from rich progressives: Mrs. A. M. Kalmykova ("the Bucket"); the unknown behind "the California Gold Mine"; the millionaire Morozov. But defeat and factional backbiting began to discourage these devotees. Moreover, though Lenin had always diverted every possible ruble to his own faction, however illegally, the continuous defection of Otzovists and others began to cut off his sources.

It was at this time, then, that Lenin resorted to "expropriations"—in cruder terms, bank robberies. The most effective of these were organized by the hitherto obscure Georgian Bolshevik Joseph Stalin and his half-crazed agent Kamo.

The whole business got the Bolsheviks involved not merely in banditry but with actual bandit elements. "In Russia," wrote Mikhail Bakunin, "the robber is the only true revolutionary. . . . The robbers in the woods, in the cities and in the villages, robbers all over Russia, and robbers imprisoned in the innumerable jails throughout the country make up one, indivisible, closely linked world—the world of the Russian revolution. . . . He who wishes to plot revolution in earnest in Russia, he who desires a popular revolution, must enter this world." As Leonard Schapiro has noted, all Russian socialists of every faction knew this world, but almost all of them, except for Lenin, recoiled from it in horror. He alone was prepared to use it: "Party members should not be measured by the narrow standard of petty bourgeois snobbery. Sometimes a scoundrel is useful to our party, precisely because he is a scoundrel."

It was in something of the same spirit that Lenin used the crudest and most abusive (though not obscene) language in his political controversies, and was fond of condemning revolutionaries who preserved the amenities of debate as people who wrongly thought the Revolution was "like a girls' school." It does not appear that this attitude was really natural to Lenin. He seems, rather, to have convinced himself that not to be abusive was a sign of lack of real commitment. But when Stalin, in 1923, was rude to Lenin's own wife, he took offense and demanded an instant apology or "the severance of relations between us"!

The Menshevik majority in the 1906 Congress had forbidden the "expropriations" (and many Bolsheviks took their side on this issue). But Lenin took powerful illicit action contrary to the Party decisions. The Central Committee, with its Menshevik majority, was answered by Lenin's capture of a small "Military-Technical Bureau" set up to cover "defensive" action against right-wing terror. In addition he set up a totally secret and, from the Party point of view, illegal Finance and Military Affairs Committee. To this all the Bolshevik funds were diverted, and Lenin used it once more to build up an apparatus from the top downward, devoted to himself and his policies. He continued with the expropriations, and it was largely with this money and apparatus that he had regained control of the majority of delegates at the Fifth Congress in 1907. But even the Fifth Congress, where he prevailed on most questions, voted him down on expropriations by 170 to 35, with 52 abstentions.

The funds had come not only from expropriations. Large legal sums intended for the Party as a whole never reached it, as in the disgraceful affair of the Schmidt sisters. Their rich brother had left his money to the Social Democratic Party, and to make sure that it got into Bolshevik hands Lenin arranged that the "legal heirs," Schmidt's two sisters, were seduced by, or married to, suitable Bolsheviks. One of these handed over his share only after threats of murder, but in the end Lenin had the money.

When the breach between Bogdanov and Lenin took place, the stories both of the more recent expropriations and of the Bolshevik mishandling of money intended for the whole Party came out. In 1910 a confidential committee of the Second International made Lenin hand over the money.[4] A "court of honor" of the Russian Social Democrats also ordered a clean-up. In 1911, Lenin not having honored its decision, Martov published the evidence.

With this, Lenin, for the sake of money, much of which he was unable to keep, was disgraced in the eyes of many already alienated by the "Tatar-Mongolian savagery" (as Rosa Luxemburg put it) of his political tactics. And anyone who imagines that the Bolsheviks at this stage were simply a devoted brotherhood of idealists should note that underground members of long standing included such names as Stalin, L. M. Kaganovich, L. Mekhlis, M. F. Shkiryatov, and G. G. Yagoda—men, in their different ways, as revolting as almost any that have been seen in this century. Nor (as might be expected) did the continual erosion of people who did not agree with Lenin fail to lower the intellectual standard of the Party considerably. This is not to say there were not men of fine intellect devotedly attached to the Bolsheviks. But among its lesser adherents there were men of very limited character and sense. Even in the small Central Committee itself, by 1912, we find such men as Sergo Ordzhonikidze, a semieducated medical orderly.

Nor were there many Bolsheviks left. Only five or six Bolshevik Committees were operating in all Russia in 1909, and Trotsky estimated total Social Democratic Party membership (*all factions*) in 1910 as ten thousand

[4] From the point of view of the International, Lenin was an obstinate troublemaker (though not the only one: on at least one occasion they found in his favor). But in general all the foreign leaders, left and right, regarded Lenin's faction struggle as a nuisance. Bebel, whom Lenin much respected, lectured him severely on his accusations against Plekhanov.

—probably an overestimate. But as the revolutionary movement withered and decayed, Lenin consolidated, on his old principle of 1902: "The smallest possible number of the most homogeneous possible groups should lead the movement, past masters in the business of professional revolution-making."[5]

At a meeting of the Central Committee in 1910 the Leninists obtained satisfaction on questions of principle, but all organizational decisions were in favor of the "Conciliators," a new set of deviationist Bolsheviks who were working for Party unity. This, to his mind, would mean the end of his control, and of the type of party he wanted. To offer conciliation at this point was particularly dangerous to his concepts. It was not merely a matter of finance: his reputation for even moderate political honesty vis-à-vis the rest of the Party was now so heavily compromised that there was little prospect of his being able to manipulate or maneuver within that sphere again.

While insisting on doctrinal purity for members of the Bolshevik faction, Lenin had previously said that this was not necessary for membership of the Social Democratic Party as a whole. In 1912, however, he assembled a Bolshevik Conference and out of the blue declared his faction to be "the Party."

It may be noted that Lenin's insistence on organizational splits, culminating in this final breach, runs contrary to the acceptance by Marx and Engels of the unification of the various wings of German Social Democracy. Engels even urged, in Lenin's youth, that in Russia the Marxist and Populist types of revolutionary socialist could be brought together in one party. Their doctrinal differences were indeed hardly greater than those within the united parties approved by the founders of Marxism.

[5] *Letter to a Comrade about Our Organizational Tasks*, in *Collected Works*, V, 189.

But Lenin's overriding motive was, in his own phrase, "Better less, but better," under his own definition of "better." As he persuasively argued,

> In the period of the decisive triumph of the counter-revolution . . . the force of circumstances has pre-scribed the following task for all party activity: to preserve the party organization created in the years when the enthusiasm of the proletarian struggle was at its highest, despite the efforts of reaction, and during the deep decline of the proletarian class struggle. . . ."[6]

None of this diverted Lenin from longer-term strategic plans. It was now, for example, that he seriously thought over how to exploit in a joint struggle against Tsarism that "bourgeois nationalism" which had produced many local uprisings in 1905 and 1906. He was virtually the only revolutionary to consider this important potential source of temporary allies.

For this, he turned largely to the "wonderful Georgian" whom he had coopted to the Central Committee in 1912—his eventual successor Joseph Stalin, easily the most able of the leading non-Russian Bolsheviks, who had first come to Lenin's notice as the organizer of the more remarkable "expropriations." Lenin's newly developing view of imperialism automatically cast the colonial peoples—of Russia as of the other imperialist states—as enemies of the great centers of capitalism. The idea of using bourgeois democratic forces in those countries as allies of the advanced proletariats against their own bourgeoisie was implicit in this analysis. Lenin's tactical solution of the nationality problem was, in effect, to give all such groups every possible promise of national independence, or at the very least autonomy. In this he was strongly opposed by many left wingers, including Rosa Luxemburg, who urged that proletarian international-

[6] *Collected Works*, XIV, 99.

ism—Marx's old idea that "the proletariat has no country"—should be the basis of socialist policy. At the time
of the Revolution, Lenin came out flatly for the right
to independence of the peripheral areas of the Russian
Empire without conditions. But at the same time, he
urged that the proletarian party in each of these countries should work against the exercise of this right, and
persuade the nations to unite in a federal system. A
certain contradiction arose here, to be most marked in
such events as the invasion of Poland in 1920 by a
Russian Army having among its baggage a Polish Communist government.

But even in those colonial and "semicolonial" areas
where there was no question of the Russian bayonet's
coming into play, such as the British and French pos-
sessions, cooperation between the Communist movements and the local bourgeois independence movements
was always fraught with contradictions. And the sub-
sequent history of many of these areas is marked by the
frequent failure of such cooperation because of Communist attempts to seize the leadership and destroy their
bourgeois allies. All the same, Lenin's instinct to exploit
every weakness in his enemy was a sound one and of at
least some help to the Revolution.

For the time being, all such considerations were
merely theoretical. In 1912, the new separate Bolshevik
Party was a small defeated sect. As V. M. Molotov told
Milovan Djilas, "The First World War found our Party
in a very weak state, its organization not connected but
scattered, and with a small membership." But for Lenin
this was, of course, as we have seen, a strong argument
for closing the ranks, cutting out dead wood, forming a
party which, however small, was totally devoted and cut
off as far as possible from the temptations of other
groups. Once again, as in 1903, Lenin had a small, tight
band of followers. Little advantage seemed to have
accrued. But now he had had nearly twenty years' experience of faction and organization, of revolution and

counterrevolution. He had honed and perfected his techniques and his ideas. He had established a powerful if ambiguous reputation in the revolutionary movement, and among his own followers his ascendancy was overwhelming.

Imperialist War and *Imperialism*

vi

Bolshevik weakness in the first years of the second decade of our century was modified by two things. One was immediate and made their new legal paper *Pravda* possible: a windfall inherited by two young Bolshevik sons of a Kazan millionaire. The other, far more important, was merely potential. Over the Stolypin years a second great industrialization boom swept Russia. The Mensheviks had in general secured the leadership of the now experienced older proletariat; a new working class, straight out of the countryside, without organization, was virgin ground for the extreme propaganda. It is customary in Communist histories to speak of a new "upsurge" in 1912–1914. While this is a great exaggeration, there were at least many strikes and general signs that the apathy of the past few years was coming to an end.

On the other hand, the regime, after the combination of repression and reform that had marked the aftermath of 1905, was now entering a period of political moderation and social advance. The new Stolypin constitution, as Lenin himself said, was "by no means a cardboard or comic-opera constitution." A great school expansion was under way which should have brought compulsory primary education up to the British level by 1922, and eliminated illiteracy by 1930. In 1912 came social insurance laws against sickness and accident, covering virtually all industrial workers. In 1913 there was a general amnesty for political offenders.

It was still true that Russia was the most backward and despotic of European countries. The peasantry, in spite of considerable improvement in their position, were still miserably poor. The working class, in spite of a renewed industrial boom, remained ill-paid and subject to regulations which would not have been tolerated in a Western country. The intelligentsia, though a section of it now hoped for a liberal evolution of the system, remained in general unreconciled to the regime. And at the center, the Tsar was still at heart a believer in autocracy, while he lacked the character to be a genuine and forceful autocrat. The young Tsarevich had hemophilia, and the Empress, a woman of strong character and restricted intelligence, was already falling into the hands of Rasputin, the demoniac monk who she believed could save her boy.

Still, for the moment, the new strengths of Russia were more impressive than the weaknesses. Lenin had little hope of revolution, except in what he regarded as the unlikely event of war. The Tsar and the Emperor Franz Joseph, he considered, would not give him "that pleasure." Such a formulation was a reasonable one on the face of it, but it ignored the lunatic calculations of the Austrians.

It was from Austrian territory in Galicia that Lenin was now, once again, trying to wean his representatives in Russia from continuous failure to attack the Mensheviks. In the summer of 1914, in fact, his mind was largely engaged in the fight against various attempts by the International, and by "wavering" Bolsheviks and others, to unite the Russian socialist sects.

The International organized a special commission on the unity of Russian Social Democracy. Representatives of eleven Russian groups attended, and all but Lenin's accepted a resolution on unity which called for a new unification Congress. Before it could be held, Austria had declared war on Serbia, on July 28. Within the week all Europe was at war.

The policy of the Bolsheviks in case of war was, of course, revolutionary. But so, in principle, was that of the whole International. At Congress after Congress the socialist parties had voted, at the very least, to oppose any such war.

Lenin was now shocked and incredulous at the news that the socialist parties almost everywhere had in fact supported their governments. When it emerged that the German Social Democrats had voted in the Reichstag to approve the war credits, he would not believe it; and even when their newspaper confirmed it, he thought the copy had been forged by the German General Staff.

It was this moment of shock which can be seen as finally cutting Lenin off from the old Social Democracy of Europe. Hitherto, with all his frequent qualms about individual acts of policy, he had regarded the German Social Democratic Party as the most mature, most reliable of the whole movement. They had, after all, voted down Eduard Bernstein's "revisionism." It was true that they had not expelled Bernstein from the Party, but it was common ground that the Social Democrats of the advanced countries were not expected to have the rigorous discipline of their underground colleagues in Russia. It was true that they, and the International, had often misjudged the Russian situation, on which Lenin was clear that his own opinion was infallible. But he had never yet doubted the general competence and loyalty of the other socialists in their own very different Western sphere.

He had, in fact, misunderstood Western socialism. He had taken at its face value the Marxist and revolutionary phraseology to which most of them piously adhered and had not seen that, unlike the alienated Russian revolutionary, the German Social Democratic worker was in reality largely assimilated to the society he was struggling to improve. It now appeared that, as so many Russians had been in one way or another, they were traitors, corrupted by the bourgeoisie. The shock of this discovery now led Lenin for the first time to start to assert his own authority among international socialists, a move which would eventually produce the Comintern.

Yet who were the "traitors"? In France the leader of the right-wing socialists, Jean Jaurès, had taken the strongest pacific line, while the left-wing leaders Jules Guesde and Gustave Hervé rallied strongly to the war. In Germany, Lensch and Parvus (A. L. Helphand) on the extreme left did the same, while the arch-"revisionist" Bernstein was one of the first to condemn the vote for war credits. In England, while moderate socialists like Philip Snowden and Ramsay Macdonald voted against war credits, the Marxist leader H. M. Hyndman supported the war.

Even the Russian situation was not so simple. The Bolshevik five-man Leading Committee in Paris disintegrated as two joined the French Army and one resigned. In Russia itself, the despised Mensheviks in the Duma voted as unanimously against the war credits as their Leninist opposite numbers; but Plekhanov was a "social patriot." In the international socialist movement for peace, the activists were far from forming a pool of recruits for Leninism.

With the help of various Austrian socialist "traitors" Lenin was able to get to Switzerland. There he tried to form an international movement based on his principle "Turn the imperialist war into a civil war." But, at the Zimmerwald and Kienthal conferences of socialists actively opposed to the war, revolutionary representatives such as K. G. Rakovski and Serrati especially objected to his attempt to denounce Martov as an agent of the bourgeoisie. Lenin and his friends formed "a feeble minority" and were unable to get control of the new movement.

Meanwhile, largely through his bold new adherent, worker A. M. Shlyapnikov, Lenin kept contact with the small and largely repressed Bolshevik centers in Russia. But with all this activity, he still had more spare time than had been available to him over the years of peace. As we have seen, he worked on Hegel. Above all, he turned to analyzing the phenomenon which, unforeseen by Marx, had so long postponed the Western revolution by "corrupting" the working class. 1916 saw the appearance of his most influential study, *Imperialism*. In fact, the official definition of Leninism is the "Marxism of the Imperialist Epoch."

Imperialism is far more than a demonstration that the big capitalist states are bound to go to war, that capitalism is responsible for the horrors not merely of poverty but also of war. That was, indeed, at the time of writing, a striking and serious indictment; thousands, and then millions, were eager for a theory which explained, and a program which eliminated, the horrors of the trenches.

Imperialism provided this. But it also, at last, gave Lenin's theoretical explanation of why economic and social development in late nineteenth- and early twentieth-century Europe had so markedly diverged from the Marxist pattern. As such, it was Lenin's major *theoretical* work, as *What Is to Be Done?* was his major work on revolutionary organization and tactics. Indeed, it may be thought of as an explanation—years belated—of why the organizational theory of *What Is to Be Done?* had had to be substituted for the previous reliance on the general proletarian movement, of why the "inevitable" trend to Marxist revolution could no longer be relied on.

The factor Marx had not foreseen was the competitive expansion into Asia and Africa of the great capitalist powers. Mere "exploitation" in general of the colonial territories, such as had occurred in previous centuries by plunder, tribute, and so on, was inadequate to the Marxist scheme. To explain the continued expansion and flourishing of capitalism as such, it was necessary to assert—and Lenin now asserted—that the basic capitalist interest in the colonial territories consisted in the export of fixed capital, which could employ colonial labor at minimal cost and thus earn "superprofits."

This gave, too, a theoretical basis to a characteristic Lenin attitude—as indeed it had been to some degree Marx's too—that the workers were always being "betrayed"; that is, the chosen class was continually showing total ineptitude in choosing leaders. The Leninist theory of imperialism stated that the gradualist elements of the working class were being "bribed" by the "superprofits," part of which the capitalists found suitable to channel to the proletariat, or at any rate a section of it, thus avoiding Marx's prediction of "increasing misery." It is not clear in what sense this could possibly apply to the non-Leninist socialists of Russia, who suffered the same persecution as that visited on the Bolsheviks.

Much of Lenin's argument was not original, as he himself generously admitted. As he said, he drew a good deal of it from the English Liberal J. A. Hobson, whose book *Imperialism* he had read twelve years earlier and had started to translate. On this view, in any case, the capitalists, in fact, were forced to turn increasingly to the export of capital to backward countries, "where," as Lenin puts it, "profits are usually high, for capital is scarce, the price of land is relatively low, wages are low, raw materials are cheap." In no sense was this a true account of the economic development of the colonial territories. Capital was not exported to them on any great scale. On the contrary—as indeed Communists have frequently pointed out—very little investment went into increasing the industrial output of Asia and Africa: the industrialized countries in fact enormously extended their own production, and their export of goods increased far more rapidly than any export of capital. British foreign investments, in fact, involved virtually no net outflow of capital, being financed from the reinvestment of profits. The French colonies imported more than they exported. Nor did the major investments in colonial countries in fact produce "superprofits"; the Rand mines, for example, gave an average annual return of not over 4.1 per cent.

Lenin explicitly linked imperialism with the unavoidable internal pressures of capitalism. He asserted that if these internal difficulties could be mastered, imperialism would be unnecessary and capitalism could solve its problems:

> It goes without saying that if capitalism could develop agriculture, which today lags far behind industry everywhere, if it could raise the standard of living of the masses who are everywhere still poverty-stricken and under-fed, in spite of the amazing advance in technical knowledge, there could be no talk of a superfluity of capital. . . . The necessity of exporting capital arises from the fact that in a few countries, capitalism has become "over-ripe" and (owing to the backward state of agriculture and the impoverished state of the masses) capital cannot find "profitable" investments.

Of course, he denied that this evolution of capitalism was possible. It has since taken place.

Lenin defined imperialism as "moribund capitalism," or as "parasitic or decaying capitalism." It was, in fact, capitalism "at its highest historical stage of development . . . on the eve of the social revolution." As the form of capitalism which had reached a dead end internally, and so was forced to another but slightly postponed dead end in the colonies, he argued that in a period of the concentration of capital and the increase of monopoly, as against (and by the winners of) the free or freeish competition of Marx's time, "finance capital" in the form of the banks had merged with and assumed control of the old "industrial capital." (In fact there was no important degree of merger between finance and industrial capital in, for example, Britain.)

Moreover, though Lenin was especially concerned to prove that (for instance) the great German banks were behind colonial expansion in Africa, the Big Five banks in Berlin not long before the war had actually submitted a confidential memorandum to their government arguing against such expansion. The German companies involved in the African countries were, in the main, get-rich-quick concerns obtaining their funds from adventurist investors, and were both peripheral to and much disliked and distrusted by German capitalism properly speaking.

In any case, as Lenin saw it, through "finance capitalism," the disastrous results predicted as arising from the old free-for-all laws of the market were to some degree avoided or postponed. But a state was nevertheless soon reached in which the iron laws of Marxism offered no further possibility of developing production under the capitalist order. This centralized concentration, with no more internal competition to crush, had no choice but to turn outward and compete with the monopoly capitalisms of other states. In his earlier analysis of imperialism, the leading German Marxist Karl Kautsky, noting that capitalists within the individual states had shown enough sense of their own self-interest to evade the destruction expected from excessive competition, suggested that they might go one stage further and also equally evade the mutual throat-cutting between national capitalisms postulated by Lenin to lead to their fall.

Lenin makes no attempt to *prove* that the capitalist states could not move on to a supranational supercartel, as Kautsky suggested. The immediate empirical evidence, indeed, made it obvious that, from the Leninist point of view, the capitalist states were *at present* engaged in a series of clashes. But so would earlier evidence have shown the same of the economic clashes between rival groups *within* given states before monopoly capitalism had been achieved. In neither case could this guarantee, even on the neo-Marxist assumptions, that when the war was over a settlement might not be reached. Such a possibility could not be faced, since the Leninist argument was now that, since poverty had not eventuated on a scale bound to lead to the collapse of capitalism, war on a scale to produce equal disruption and suffering, and hence equally revolutionary situations, *must* do duty. For what else would serve?

In general Lenin's whole thesis is defective both evidentially and logically.[1] But it retains, if not its validity, at least its popularity. This is natural enough. For, like so much Marxist and other doctrinal work, its value lies in purporting to provide serious and scholarly backing to a simple idea—"the advanced countries exploit the backward ones."

In fact it gains its effect in the same way that much of Marx's own economic work impresses—not because it is read or understood, but because it appears to give a scholarly and scientific justification to the purely ethi-

---

[1] Interestingly enough, the Soviet economist E. Varga pointed out after World War II that the Netherlands became *more* prosperous after losing Indonesia; one seldom sees it suggested that postwar Indonesia resembled any sort of Dutch semicolonial or neocolonial territory.

cal (and economically indefinable) notion of "surplus value"[2]—that is, to the simple and easily grasped idea that "capitalists exploit workers."

[2] When attempts were made to have the Italian Communist Party debate it seriously in the 1920s, Palmiro Togliatti (we are told by one of his then colleagues) could not be brought to show any interest: the theory was, he explained, not for economists, but for the masses. (Ignazio Silone in *Dissent*, September-October 1970.)

1917

vii

In January 1917, Lenin ended a lecture to Swiss students with the words, "We of the older generation may not see the decisive battles of this coming revolution." By mid-March the Tsarist regime had been overthrown, and eight months later the Bolsheviks were in power.

His pessimism is instructive. In fact, he saw the strengths of the Tsarist regime (as of the other European regimes) and its weaknesses were largely hidden from him.

At the beginning of the war he had expected a great revolutionary upsurge of class-consciousness from the masses, in Russia as elsewhere. Instead they as well as their leaders—more than their leaders—had given way to patriotic moods. Even after more than two years of frightful fighting, the mass armies had nowhere collapsed. The Russian soldier, though in general losing ground, had shown his traditional fortitude and endurance. No doubt the country, like all Europe, was war-weary in a general sense, but there was little overt sign of it. The besetting weaknesses of supply and production had been largely overcome, and the few thousand Bolsheviks remained uninfluential, little more than a force in being.

The weaknesses hidden from, or not grasped by, Lenin were not among the masses but at the center. Since early 1914, under the influence of the Empress, herself under the spell of the charlatan Rasputin, an able and self-confident political leadership had been replaced by sluggish servility. "The fish begins to stink at its head." It was in circles close to the ruling camarilla, among the establishment liberals, among serious patriots and angry intriguers alike, that it had come to be felt that methods of rule were becoming intolerable. In spite of the assassination of Rasputin at the end of 1916, the Empress still exercised a baleful influence. Serfs of the palace, rather than stalwart defenders of the monarchy, held most of the key posts of power.

In this atmosphere, in March 1917 avoidable food shortages in Petrograd led to strikes and rioting, and the third-line troops of the Petrograd garrison refused to fire on the rioters. The Tsar's army commanders refused him their support for any attempt to preserve his tottering throne, and in a week the three-hundred-year-old dynasty had gone forever. Lenin's first comment on these events was that it was the work of the Allied embassies, using the liberal politicos and the generals, because they feared Nicholas might make a separate peace with Germany.

Though this was hardly true, it did contain the important point that the Revolution was a national one, with a program of popular war against Germany. There was no sign at all of the defeatism or proletarian internationalism which, in theory, should have preceded and caused the Revolution. In fact, the February Revolution, like that of 1905, took the revolutionary parties by surprise, and they played almost no part in it. The new Provisional Government set up by a self-appointed committee of the Duma had virtually no claim to legitimacy. The newly emerging Petrograd Soviet, under moderate control until the autumn, wielded as much power on the spot. Still, unlike 1905, there was now naturally a spirit of cooperation between all the bodies and parties which had inherited Russia.

Unlike the soviets of 1905, which had genuinely emerged out of the working class as strike committees, and never lost their character as workers' organs, the 1917 soviets consisted largely of coopted socialist intellectuals of various factions. Political party leaders such as Lenin and V. M. Chernov managed to get seats on them immediately on their return from exile. In March 1917, already only 7 of the 42 members of the Executive Committee of the crucial Petrograd Soviet were workers (though it is true that an inordinate representation was given to soldiers' deputies).

Men of high principles and low experience, the new rulers took a number of steps to ensure the eventual collapse of order. The Provisional Government's deal with the Petrograd Soviet included the promise that the mutinous troops would be neither disarmed nor sent to the front. Discipline was an insoluble problem from then on; and a force existed whose sole *raisons d'être* were to draw pay and to place itself at the disposal of whatever party could best appeal to it. For the moment, the soldiers' mood remained patriotic, and Lenin was heartily booed for the speech he made on his arrival in April; but their moods and aspirations could change. Moreover, they were considerably less experienced politically even than the workers.

The new Premier, Prince Georgi Lvov, from the noblest liberal motives, went on to dismantle the entire administrative and police framework of the country without putting anything remotely effective in its place. Throughout Russia the alleged organs of government were councils and committees amounting largely to self-appointed debating societies for liberals and socialists. These were everywhere complemented by the soviets, which, to start with, were equally self-appointed debating societies, though for socialists only—but having, at least, Party contacts and organizations within an important section of the population. As soon as the Bolsheviks could gain control of these latter, by the various tactics of committee maneuver at which they were so experienced, they would dispose of at least some elements of power against everybody else's none.

The history of the revolutionary year 1917 is one of great intricacy. It will be sufficient for our purposes to indicate the cruxes in Lenin's handling, first of the Party leadership, once again proving balky on every important occasion, and then of the whole political situation.

Cut off at first in Switzerland, he only managed to negotiate a passage through Germany in the famous "sealed train" in time to arrive in Petrograd on April 16. This German cooperation in forwarding him and his colleagues to Russia naturally aroused much hostile comment, and over the following period the cry that he was a "German agent" was one of the most effective elements in anti-Bolshevik propaganda.

His political assets at this moment lay mainly in the following he had built up in the past seventeen years and the experience he had gained, if not of mass movements, at least of the attitudes and tendencies of the revolutionary parties whose leaders were now his only obstacle to power. He was a figure barely, if at all, known to the masses, but he was famous (if not always favorably so) among the revolutionary intelligentsia. And even though he remained somewhat suspect to a number of the most energetic and extremist among the revolutionists, he was to offer them the only political organization standing for the total and immediate over-throw of "capitalism."

The main efforts of the past few years had been in building up a small but devoted and energetic group of "professional revolutionaries." As the factory workers and soldiers turned to the various purveyors of political ideas which they themselves lacked, these professionals did not by any means have it their own way. At first the moderates easily dominated the elections to the soviets. Nevertheless, the Bolshevik hard core had picked up, and were passing on to their subordinates, the Leninist technique of ceaseless organization, penetration of committees, and so forth. The methods which Lenin had used on a small scale in the intra-Party struggle were now to be applied to the factories and the regiments in Petrograd.

But first the Party itself had to be mastered. Lenin had created a cadre of Leninists. They had accepted all his decisions, and had grown used to accepting them. For them, he was the *Starik*—the old man—and had been since his twenties; for him they were a machinery for transmitting and imposing his own views.

But there was an important difficulty. His followers did not think of themselves as simply extensions of his will. In theory, every Party decision was taken democratically by a Central Committee or Congress, however packed. All the members of these thought of themselves not as intellectual serfs but as men who voted on an issue's merits. No doubt, by 1917, the Bolshevik leadership consisted entirely of men who had hitherto carried out Lenin's line, in spite of occasional qualms. The trouble was that in each new situation there was no way of telling what that line was going to be. No set of Leninist principles—or at least none which any of his leading followers was able to master—existed by which they could arrive at or anticipate his own conclusions. In the vast events of the next five years, Lenin again and again made his private and often surprising decision first and then, before putting it into action, had to overcome the resistance and reluctance of his leading operatives.

Now in his absence, the Party leadership (at this point effectively in the hands of Kamenev and Stalin) had taken the view that the bourgeois revolution would last a long time; that the role of the Party was to put "pressure on the Provisional Government" to induce it to accept peace terms, since the slogan "Down with the war" was useless; and that discussions or unification with the Mensheviks should now start. These propositions were voted for by an All-Russian Bolshevik Party Conference, held just before Lenin's arrival.

Lenin had different—indeed opposite—views. In his *Letters from Afar*, written in March, he had in effect called for the seizure of power by the "proletariat" (for the time being he rejected the soviets themselves, which in 1905 he had thought of as revolutionary organs). On his arrival he put forward a clear program of no support for the government, no unification with the Mensheviks, peace to be the result only of the overthrow of capitalism, and an immediate socialist revolution. *Pravda* immediately disowned his view; Kamenev, Alexei Rykov, and others led the opposition to it. A joint Bolshevik/Menshevik bureau was even set up to prepare for unification (while in the countryside, as late as the autumn, there were still twenty-eight local branches in which the two groups remained united).

Lenin once again, by the use of his personal authority, and by a slight tactical compromise, won the Party over (in particular at the Seventh All-Russian Party Conference in May), this time to the formula of seizure of power by the soviets once the Bolsheviks had a majority in them. He was still blocked on some issues, receiving not a single vote for a proposition to break finally with the Second International: but he generally reasserted his control and changed the Party's direction.

On July 16 and 17 came what may be thought of as the Bolsheviks' first attempt to seize power, though that is to put it in a more clear-cut fashion than it appeared at the time. In fact, the technique of seizing power, the mere mechanics of revolution, had not yet been properly worked out. A large and disorderly armed demonstration was organized calling on the Petrograd Soviet to take power. It seems to have been a sort of reconnaissance which, it was hoped, would turn into a general assault. The move, resembling some of the Jacobin insurrections of the 1790s, was a failure. When Lenin got another chance, he was not to rely again on this disorganized, semi-spontaneous mass action.

With the failure of the coup, the tide turned against the Bolsheviks. The other parties at last began to see, in however reluctant and inadequate a fashion, that there might be enemies on the left as well as on the right. The government now sought the prosecution of the Bolshevik leaders on the grounds of the receipt of German money.

For once again, money was a major concern of the Bolsheviks, and large funds were absolutely vital to the establishment of the professional Party and the Party press on the big scale now required. Though the evidence for a trickle of German money previous to the February Revolution is dubious (some money seems to have been allotted by the Germans for such purposes but to have fallen almost entirely into the hands of crooked intermediaries), after April it is clearly established that German funds reached the Bolsheviks on a large scale. (Lenin specifically denied that he or the Party had any dealings with the two main contact men of the Germans. However, two letters of this period actually published in Russia in 1923 show that these contacts did exist.) Of course, there was no question whatever of Lenin's "being in German pay" in the sense of carrying out their instructions or being influenced by them in any way. For the moment, he and they had the same immediate aim, the overthrow of the Russian government and Army. Each was using the other. But naturally the mere acceptance of the money was not easy for the Russian public to swallow. The Bolsheviks denied it, and Lenin went into hiding in Finland.

There, perhaps feeling that his chances of coming to power were now greatly lessened, he set to work on his *State and Revolution*. This, coming when it does, is one of the most extraordinary and revealing of all his writings. It is not (as much of his earlier work had been) any sort of guide to political tactics but an expression of the most purely Utopian and theoretical side of the Marxist doctrine of society. While Petrograd simmered in the background, Lenin—right on the eve of the anticipated and actual seizure of power—was giving the most idyllic semianarchist account of proletarian revolution and of how it is to result immediately in the most intensive democratization, culminating in the withering away of the state. On every point he was to do the opposite within months, and even at the time the book had an air of being totally inapplicable to the Bolshevik situation.

The thesis presented in *State and Revolution* is far from an ignoble one. In the long run, for many people, the appeal of communism lies precisely in the idea that it is possible for a modern industrialized culture to operate without any machinery of compulsion, and without narrow (or any) specialization. And Lenin, in rejecting the anarchist idea that this could come into being immediately after a revolution, appeared to remove the stigma of utopianism from it. At the same time, by suggesting that it could be realized *fairly* soon, and that the process could at least begin immediately, he avoided the appearance of postponing the good society indefinitely, and of thus giving the impression that its image would in practice serve as little more than a pie-in-the-sky inducement to accept unpleasant realities.

The central theme was, in fact, that "the proletarian state will begin to wither away immediately after its victory," and even while it lasted, since it would be supported by the overwhelming mass of the population, it could enforce its will "almost without any special machinery." (When Bukharin raised the question of the state withering away at the Seventh Party Congress, in March 1918, Lenin had no patience with him, saying, "One may well wonder when the state will begin to wither away. . . . To proclaim this withering away in advance is to violate historical perspective.")

State and Revolution has been described by Dr. Karl Wittfogel as the most "hypocritical" of Lenin's works on the grounds that in his account of the Marxist view of the state Lenin wholly ignores Marx's "Asiatic" form, in which a centralized, noncapitalist, nonland-owner, bureaucratic autocracy rules. It is true enough that such a conception comes much closer to the Soviet regime as finally established than does any conception of democracy or the withering state. But it seems clear that there was no "hypocrisy." As far as the "Asiatic" form was concerned, Lenin doubtless thought it irrelevant to a European and capitalist heritage. In any case, the booklet was not published before the Revolution, so there can be no question of its being a piece of intellectual demagogy. It did not come out until the spring of 1918, by which time the new secret police had been in action for months. It is not anything so crude as hypocrisy, surely, that we see here, but rather the paradoxes, the ambivalence, of Lenin's whole political nature.

Before he could finish the book, things swung back the Bolshevik way. In early September, the new Commander-in-Chief, Lavr Kornilov, moved to establish a military dictatorship, if possible in alliance with the moderate left. Once it became clear that the Bolsheviks sought a monopoly of power, the only force in the country capable of preventing them would have been such a military intervention. But it now presented itself to Alexander Kerensky, the current Prime Minister, and to his socialist and democratic colleagues, as a matter of Reaction versus Revolution.

Moreover, lacking any reliable force of its own, the government was compelled to rely on Bolshevik armed organizations in stopping Kornilov (though we should note that a key role was played by the Menshevik-controlled Railwaymen's Union). And with the elimination of Kornilov, virtually no other centers of power but that of the Bolsheviks survived.

There now came, moreover, a certain revival of the sentimental solidarity of the socialists and revolutionaries in general as old and now victorious comrades, whatever the differences and disagreements which had so shaken them in July. Even then, although a number of the more sensible Mensheviks and SR's—for example, Irakli Tseretelli and Boris Savinkov—realized the danger, it had been psychologically impossible for most of them to grasp for long the idea of a real enemy on the left, or to press home (as their critics now understandably say they should have) the charges against the Bolsheviks.

At the end of September, Lenin demanded the immediate seizure of power. The view found no support in the Central Committee. Once again, over the following weeks, he had to exert all his authority. It was only on October 23 that he finally won his majority in the Committee. Even now Kamenev and Zinoviev were so strongly opposed to the idea that they denounced it publicly. Lenin was understandably enraged and branded them as traitors.

The extreme weakness of the authorities, the disappearance of both the machinery of administration and the prestige and credibility of the Provisional Government, were obvious enough. It may seem surprising that so few of the leading Bolsheviks saw this as Lenin did. But there seem to have been two main reasons.

First they, like so many members of the other socialist parties, did not want the stigma of committing political fratricide. And second, they doubted the capacity of the Bolsheviks to lead the country and to hold the power that was there for the asking. These doubts are understandable. Even Lenin was quite clear about the possibility of Bolshevik collapse.

The realignment within the revolutionary movement during the course of 1917 had had the striking and more or less accidental result of compensating for the timidity and lack of élan to be found among the Leninist devotees. While many of these (not only Zinoviev and Kamenev) showed little enthusiasm for the seizure of power, much of the missing revolutionary energy was supplied by men who had in one way or another previously rejected what they regarded as the authoritarian centralism of the Leninist conception of the Party. The outstanding example was Trotsky himself, but the Trotsky group in general acted and voted similarly (and former Mensheviks were also among the most vigorous revolutionaries: for example Vladimir Antonov-Ovseenko, who carried out the arrest of the Provisional Government). And Lenin, over the following years, was able to make Trotsky's new acquiescence in "democratic centralism," arising in the first place simply in the course of gravitating toward extreme revolutionary policies, into a permanent thing.

It is clear from the reports of the October 23 Central Committee meeting that the idea of the rising was "not popular," that "the masses received our call with bewilderment." Even the reports from most of the garrisons were tepid. But there was to be no nonsense about mass demonstrations this time. The seizure of power, in fact, was to be an almost purely military operation, carried out by a small number of Red Guards, only partly from the factories, and a rather larger group of Bolshevized soldiery.

It is not clear, in view of the rather unsatisfactory

nature of elections to the soviets, and Bolshevik skill in committee-fiddling, just how much and how fervent support they really had among the workers. The main unions (as Bolshevik writers tell us) were under Menshevik control until the October Revolution. (*After* the Bolshevik victory, the elections to the Constituent Assembly in November 1917 make it plain that the Bolsheviks had won, for the time being, the bulk of the working-class vote in the cities, with the Mensheviks deservedly at their lowest ebb.)

It is clear indeed that the Bolsheviks already had a fair measure of support in October 1917, but it is equally clear that a great part of that support went to them as the party working to give political power to the soviets, and this did not in most minds imply one-party rule. Even many of the Central Committee majority, and the great bulk of the Bolshevik rank and file, supported the insurrection with a view to installing not so much a Party dictatorship as soviet rule and a socialist coalition government.

On November 7, at the urgent insistence of Lenin that even a day's delay might be fatal, the Party seized power. As David Mitchell says in his *1919: Red Mirage,* "The Bolsheviks had not captured a Ship of State, they had boarded a derelict." Their major difficulties were ahead of them, not behind them.

On November 8 Lenin presented the newly assembled Second Congress of Soviets with a *fait accompli* in the form of a new government, the Council of People's Commissars, all Bolsheviks, with himself at its head. He was right. From the action of the railway trade unions and other bodies, and even of the majority of his own first Council of People's Commissars, we can be fairly sure that but for Lenin's tactics the Congress would have voted for a coalition of socialist parties. It is of course arguable that such a regime would have lacked both stability and grip, and that in the current state of disintegration some sort of single-minded dictatorship was inevitable.

There were still great obstacles to the establishment of one-party rule. The Executive Committee of the Railwaymen's Union initiated an attempt to form a socialist coalition. Since its big role in the struggle against Kornilov, the union had emerged as a major political force. Now, apart from anything else, the outcome of a final attempt by Kerensky to march on Petrograd depended a great deal on its good will. It demanded a coalition of all the socialist parties on pain of a general railway strike. On November 11 the Bolshevik Central Committee (with Lenin and Trotsky absent) unanimously voted in favor of such a government. Negotiations were immediately undertaken, with Kamenev as the leading Bolshevik delegate. On November 14 Lenin, after failing to get a majority vote in the Central Committee for suspending the talks, fell back on a negotiating position clearly unacceptable to the other parties.

When the negotiations petered out—Kerensky having meanwhile been repulsed—on November 18 Kamenev, Rykov, and three others resigned from the Central Committee and from the Council of People's Commissars (together with eight People's Commissars who were not also members of the CC) on the grounds that all working-class parties—that is, all parties represented in the soviets—should be brought into the government: "Other than this there is only one policy: the preservation of a purely Bolshevik government by means of political terror."

Lenin played for time, consolidated his power, and admitted a few "Left" Social Revolutionaries to his government on December 1. By the end of the month the threat to his rule had faded away and the erring Bolsheviks had submitted. Lenin again readmitted Kamenev and the others to leadership. One of the motives for

Lenin's frequent forgiveness of these erring figures seems to have been the enormous difficulty he found among the Bolsheviks of laying his hands on even mediocre executants of his will. The Party and state had to be ruled somehow. If those who opposed him in 1917 (and 1918) had been removed, the already imperfect instrument would have been severely weakened.

After November 7 there was for a time no other authority than Lenin's throughout most of Russia. The workers, who had been comparatively apathetic toward the idea of the seizure of power, now for some months —and this is the only time in Russian history for which this is true—became in their majority firm supporters of the Bolsheviks; only the unions of the skilled workers remained Menshevik.

If Lenin had agreed to the demand by Kamenev and others to make the new government a coalition of all the socialist parties, stability, unity, and peace might perhaps have been achieved—with a firm majority in the Constituent Assembly, whose urgent convocation was one of the Bolshevik promises. One of Lenin's charges against Kerensky had been that elections to this body had been too long postponed. He actually declared to the Congress of Soviets:

> As a democratic government we cannot ignore the will of the people even if we disagree with it. In the acid test of reality . . . the peasants will soon find out by themselves where the truth was. And even if the peasants continue to follow the Socialist Revolutionaries, even if they give that party the majority in the Constituent Assembly, we will say: so be it.

He evidently calculated that the "Decree on Land" he had just put through, by which (without consulting his colleagues) he abandoned the Bolshevik and took over the Social Revolutionary principle of land distribution, would win over the peasants. But in the elections which followed, they still voted for the party which had consistently fought for their interests. According to Lenin's own figures, the Bolsheviks got just over nine million votes, the Social Revolutionaries nearly twenty-one million and liberal groups over four and a half million.

When the Constituent Assembly, for which all Russia's revolutionaries and liberals had worked for nearly a century, met in January 1918, it was simply dissolved by force.

Lenin in Power

VIII

Lenin's most urgent problem was the continuing German advance. The new regime completed the disintegration of the Army which its predecessors had begun. Units were at this time efficient almost precisely to the degree that they had not come under Bolshevik influence and control. To destroy any further prospect of military action against the Soviet government, and at the same time to gain further support among the soldiery, automatically involved progressively breaking the Army. The new Commander-in-Chief, who refused orders to negotiate an armistice, was dismissed and lynched.

On December 15 an armistice was signed, and the front-line soldiery trickled off back to the villages in ever-increasing numbers.

Peace negotiations with the Germans now began at Brest-Litovsk. Almost immediately a new struggle started inside the Bolshevik Party.

At a conference held in the last days of the year, 32 votes were cast in favor of a revolutionary war against Germany, 16 for an absurd formulation of Trotsky's "Neither war nor peace," and only 15 in favor of Lenin's insistence on "peace at any price." The German terms, put in January, involved an enormous loss of territory. The Central Committee now met and accepted Trotsky's view by 9 votes to 7. Lenin's position was weakened partly because he had never ceased to declare that the Bolsheviks alone could conclude a general peace settlement as against one between Russia and Germany alone. His doctrine through 1917 had been that there would be no separate peace: by fraternization, by appeal to all the peoples for a general peace, and if necessary by revolutionary war, permanent peace and socialism could be established in Europe.

Lenin justified the Bolshevik seizure of power, in spite of an inadequate proletariat, by the concept that this was simply breaking "the weakest link" in the chain of capitalist states, and would help to produce the similar revolutions in the West which would make the Russian Revolution itself viable and (retrospectively) justifiable. When he took power he believed, from various minor troubles in Germany and elsewhere, that "a turning point is at hand, we are on the eve of a world-wide revolution." He still held that revolution in the other advanced countries was necessary if the Bolsheviks were to succeed. But meanwhile Europe was, after all, still unripe. The prospect of revolutionary war with few and demoralized troops against a German Army at the height of its confidence and power was a chimera. Moreover, even if great reserves of revolutionary patriotism could be unleashed, as Bukharin thought, the generalized revolutionary and patriotic euphoria would itself endanger one-party Bolshevik rule. Lenin saw clearly enough that the Germans simply could not now be opposed. They resumed their advance.

Lenin now once again threatened to resign unless his

views were met. By every conceivable pressure, he finally got a Central Committee majority in favor of peace of 7 to 4 with 4 abstentions, and the Treaty of Brest-Litovsk was signed on March 3. But the division in the Party had gone so far that the "left" Communists who had opposed the treaty, led by Bukharin, were seriously discussing seizing power—and putting Lenin under arrest for twenty-four hours to ease the transition.

The treaty shocked Russia, Bolshevik and non-Bolshevik alike. By its vast losses of territory in the West, the country was reduced to a second-class power. Anger against the Lenin government rose strongly. Yet, as he said, all the alternatives involved the immediate collapse of Bolshevik power, while Brest-Litovsk merely put it into grave risk and danger.

The other major difficulties that Lenin now began to face were largely, though not entirely, of his own creation. He had envisaged a phase of "temporary alliance with the whole peasantry," whom the "Decree on Land" had at least pacified, and had denounced as adventurist the idea of proceeding to socialism without a transition stage. In May 1918, he decided that this stage was complete.

He now took the view that the triumph of socialism could be achieved in a few months and launched the phase which came to be known as "War Communism" —though that phrase, a later invention, suggests that it was intended as a temporary and emergency policy, which is not the case. The troubles that followed were due more than anything else to this decision. Lenin himself was to say in a speech in October 1921,

> We made the mistake of deciding to change over directly to Communist production and distribution. We sought to obtain a sufficient quantity of grain from the peasants by the way of the *Razverstka* [compulsory grain delivery quotas], then to apportion it to the industries, and that thus we would obtain Communist production and distribution. I would not affirm

that this was exactly how we visualized it, but we did act in this spirit.

Throughout the country, on this basis, "Committees of Poor Peasants" were formed and, as Lenin put it, "The Soviet republic now sends detachments of armed workers, in the first place those who are the most politically advanced, from the two capitals to the countryside. These workers carry socialism to the countryside, bringing the poor peasants over to their side, organize them, enlighten them, help them to suppress the resistance of the bourgeoisie. . . ." This was probably the biggest mistake made by Lenin when in power. Brest-Litovsk and the disruption of the Army had alienated many hitherto undecided military elements and caused reactionary armed forces to spring up in the North Caucasus and elsewhere. But now alienated the mass of the peasantry was everywhere also alienated.

Two hundred and forty-five peasant risings are officially given for 1918 alone, while ninety-nine are listed in twenty provinces—about a third of Bolshevik territory—in seven months of 1919. As the Civil War spread, the White armies were generally welcomed until the peasants found that they too were, in the main, unsympathetic to peasant aspirations. But even after their defeat, peasant uprisings continued—on an even larger scale—until the introduction of the New Economic Policy in 1921.

The other characteristic of the period was a change from the system of workers' control in the factories, which had come in, rather scrappily, in the immediate post-October period, to a strictly disciplined and centralized factory system. Trotsky remarked that compulsory labor was the foundation of socialist society. Though his "labor armies" were only one form of enforcing this, labor laws became increasingly draconic through the period, culminating in labor books (the basis of Soviet labor policy ever since), penal battalions, and finally concentration camps for slackers. As Lenin put it, "The solution of this question [social justice] must be subordinated to the interests of production."[1]

It is not very clear at what stage, and in what sense, Lenin imagined Russia's social organization to be. Though, following Marx, he held that the true sign of a socialist revolution was the destruction of the state machinery (as against the reformist notion of simply taking it over), in fact much of the local machinery of the Russian state had been ruined not by the October but by the February Revolution. And now that Lenin had the power, he did not "destroy" the central organs in the form of the old ministries but took them over as intact as possible, developing (as in other spheres) the theory that bourgeois "specialists" could be made to work for the proletarian regime.

In April 1917 he had said that his aim was not the immediate "introduction" of socialism, but an "immediate transition only to the *control* by the Soviet of Workers' Deputies over the social production and distribution of products." And just before the seizure of power, he defined the "socialist" order he had in mind as "the continuation of capitalism under the workers' control."

The first steps of economic reorganization were very moderate. There was little nationalization, except where active resistance was encountered. For example, the banks were left alone for two months and were seized only when they refused to lend money to the government. Heavy industry and private railways were not nationalized until June 1918, and then, quite explicitly, on pragmatic grounds. Lenin's immediate aim was, as he said, "a sort of state capitalism." He had been much impressed by the organization of the Ger-

[1] From a speech given on March 15, 1920, in *Collected Works*, XXV, 80.

man economy in World War I (described by Professor E. H. Carr as "the first more or less fully planned national economy in modern times"), and openly put it forward as a model.

For the War Communism period, he sometimes spoke of "socialism" in being. Later, after the introduction of the New Economic Policy, it could hardly be called "socialism" and, although he still sometimes referred to "state capitalism," that lacked appeal. So the usual usage became just "Soviet Society," a term without specific meaning. His famous phrase, "Communism is nothing but Soviet rule plus the electrification of the entire country,"[2] equally lacks Marxist content.

As for the degree to which the soviets were in any case proletarian organs, Lenin put it that

> so far, we have not achieved the state where the working masses could participate in government—except on paper; there is still the cultural level, which you will never render subject to legislation. This low cultural level has the effect of making the Soviets, which according to their programme are organs of government *by the working people*, actually into organs of government *for the working people*, by the advanced elements of the proletariat, but not by the working masses.[3]

Through 1918, an increasing tempo of "red terror" swept the country, very much at Lenin's own insistence. It was directed first against the class enemy, but finally against all enemies of the Party, including hostile socialists. Lenin was always fond of speaking of the Revolution in terms of birth pangs, as Marx and Engels had done before him. His view of the horrors of birth were more extreme than theirs. He asked what woman was repelled from love and having children simply be-

[2] Speech at a Moscow Provincial Party Conference, November 21, 1920, in *Collected Works*, XXV, 491.
[3] *Collected Works*, XXIV, 145.

cause birth turns a woman into a "tortured, lacerated, pain-crazed, half-dead lump of flesh." His knowledge of childbirth, he tells us, came from the gory Zola on the one hand and from the forgotten memoirs of a forgotten doctor of the old type on the other; the idea that since the time at which they wrote medical science had already eased the lot of women does not seem to have occurred to him.

He had given a theoretical justification of terror as early as 1905, when he envisaged the use of it in the style of 1792 "to settle accounts with Tsarism" after the Revolution. In 1908 he had written of "real, nation-wide terror, which reinvigorates the country and through which the Great French Revolution achieved glory." Many similar pronouncements could be cited.

The Provisional Government had abolished the death penalty, except for military offenses. The new regime abolished it in military cases too. For some months there were no (legal) executions in Russia. But this was to prove as temporary as Lenin's similar and simultaneous promises to respect the will of the Constituent Assembly and to abolish in the immediate future the "temporary" restraints put on the press after the Revolution.

Even leading Bolsheviks noted, in the words of the majority of the People's Commissars when they resigned from the government as early as November 1917, that the rejection of a coalition government meant "government by means of political terror," while another (Emilian Yaroslavsky) denounced statements by "responsible leaders" that "for one of ours we shall kill five opponents," as part and parcel of Lenin's "regime of the bayonet and the saber."

December 20, 1917, saw the founding of the Cheka —the secret police—which under its various names has been a recognizedly important component of the regime ever since. In theory it did not at first have the right to execute. Whatever Lenin's own wishes, neither the

Party nor its supporters were yet fully prepared for a bloodbath. The mood was changed fairly gradually.

An announcement in the same month, which had branded the whole of the liberal Constitutional Democratic Party as "enemies of the people" whose leaders were "outside the law," led to the lynching of two of their ex-ministers in a Petrograd hospital on January 20, 1918. On January 27, Lenin—speaking, at this stage, about speculators only—publicly announced that they should be shot on the spot and that "we can achieve nothing unless we use terror." On February 23, *Pravda* published an announcement that the Cheka could "see no other method of fighting counterrevolutionaries, spies, speculators, looters, hooligans, saboteurs, and other parasites than their merciless destruction on the spot." On the following day the first known case of shooting without trial by the Cheka took place. As one of its leaders wrote:

Life had made it necessary to appropriate by revolutionary means the right to immediate execution. Comrade Dzerzhinsky [the first head of the secret police] had taken a step not foreseen by decree, not authorised by anyone. The left Socialist Revolutionaries, heading the Commissariat of Justice, raised a cry, demanded that the question be brought up in the Council of People's Commissars. However, Vladimir Ilyich [Lenin] declined to include this question in the agenda of the *Sovnarkom*. He realised that Comrade Dzerzhinsky was right. One cannot go against life. In this way life itself legalised the right of the Cheka to immediate execution.

For Lenin himself continually insisted on intensified terror against the judgment of many of his subordinates. For example, as early as June 1918 he intervened against the Petrograd Party's error in restraining elements who wished for mass terror: "This is unheard of! The energy and mass nature of the terror must be encouraged." In August he had similarly to call on the

Nizhni-Novgorod Soviet "to apply mass terror immediately, to execute and exterminate hundreds of prostitutes, drunken soldiers, former officers, etc." And so on. Reasons given for executions in the Soviet press included simply describing the dead man as "a cunning and crafty counter-revolutionary," or "having used his premises for intrigue against the Soviet." Others were simply down as "shot in the ordinary course of the Red Terror," or as "an ex-member of the Constitutional Democratic Party," or as "a counter-revolutionary by conviction."

The execution of the imperial family too was in fact decided by Lenin himself, as Trotsky makes clear. (One occasionally hears it said that it was politically necessary to shoot the whole family because the killing of the Tsar and the fourteen-year-old Tsarevich alone would have left the others in the succession. In fact, this is quite false: the grand duchesses had no right of succession—nor, of course, did the doctor, the nurse, or the dog, executed at the same time. But the political importance even of the Tsar at this point was negligible. In the Civil War the White authorities were to make almost no use of the monarchist principle.)

On August 30, 1918, the free-lance Social Revolutionary terrorist Fanny Kaplan put two bullets into Lenin in an assassination attempt. This raised personal as well as political issues. It may be difficult for us to conceive the moral respect hitherto inevitably given by the Russian left to a revolutionary assassin. Accounts at the time show numbers of Bolsheviks horrified at the idea that she might be executed—Krupskaya denying in tears that such a thing was possible and Lenin himself silently embarrassed. For many years it was believed that the girl had not in fact been executed: indeed, her fate was not finally confirmed until her Cheka executioner described it in passing in his memoirs published in the 1960s.

The attempt was made the occasion for a great intensification of the terror. Not all Party members had at first accepted it. Resistance came from a majority of the local soviets whose opinions were canvassed in 1918. A leading Old Bolshevik, the journalist Mikhail Olminsky, wrote several critical pieces in *Pravda* making it clear that a section of the Party opposed the extensive executions being carried out and felt that the powers of the Cheka were greatly excessive.

Prominent Chekists counterattacked Olminsky. Lenin backed them up. He attacked "a narrow-minded intelligentsia" in the Party who "sob and fuss" over mistakes made by the Cheka; adding, "When we are reproached with cruelty, we wonder how people can forget the most elementary Marxism."

The main point to be stressed is that this ruthless and doctrinaire attitude was due far more to a preconceived notion than to any careful assessment of the situation. As Professor Adam Ulam points out in his *The Bolsheviks*, "Far from being a regrettable necessity, the extent of the Bolshevik Terror was one of the factors which made their victory in the Civil War more difficult." Even the Communist Mikhail Sholokhov, in his *And Quiet Flows the Don*, shows how previously nonpolitical Don Cossacks were thrown into bitter resistance by Bolshevik atrocities.

While the bulk of the working class remained, if not as enthusiastically pro-Bolshevik as before, at least largely anti-White, Lenin's policies in the countryside, and his surrender of Russian territory at Brest-Litovsk, had nevertheless ranged the regime against most of the political and social forces in the country. That the Bolsheviks nevertheless won the Civil War must be regarded as his most extraordinary achievement. For, though we must grant Trotsky his great role in organizing and using the new Red Army, nevertheless, it was Lenin who took the main decisions and who provided the truly decisive driving force. Still, as he himself said, it was a very near thing.

While millions had served in World War I, the Civil War consisted of encounters between Red armies of several hundred thousand and rather better equipped and trained but considerably smaller White ones supported peripherally and erratically by a minor degree of Allied "intervention." Lenin's was basically a victory by a weak and widely hated group over an enemy even weaker, no less hated, and politically far less clear-headed or united. The divisions existing among the Whites were partly, it is true, due to accident and incompetence: but partly they were inherent in the whole White situation—the officer class (or such of them as went with the Whites) were virtually incapable of political collaboration in any genuine sense with the more or less legitimate representatives of the majority parties of the Constituent Assembly. In fact, for a considerable section of the officers the Bolsheviks were no worse than the anti-Bolshevik socialist parties. When Lenin's government appeared as the one strong center capable of ruling and rebuilding Russia, a good proportion of the old officers rallied to, or at least were more or less willing to serve in, the Red Army. Lenin's insistence on backing Trotsky in the use of these officers, against very strong doctrinaire opposition in the Party, perhaps made the decisive contribution to victory.

Deaths in battle were comparatively low. The Red Terror probably accounted for some half a million deaths, and the various White and nationalist terrors for perhaps half as many. The total of violent deaths over the period 1918–1920 was still perhaps no more than a million. But the disintegration of authority and the collapse of the agricultural system as a result of the procurement policies played vast havoc.

A Soviet source estimates the total excess mortality in those provinces where statistics were kept as about seven million between January 1918 and July 1920. An estimate for the remaining areas should bring this up to about nine million. These deaths were largely from typhus and famine—and the great famine of 1921 with its five-million-odd deaths was yet to come.

In this period production on the land had fallen to about half the 1913 total. Peasant risings became endemic. And, worse still from the Bolshevik point of view, the proletariat was also both shrinking and becoming alienated. By 1920, about half of the old proletariat had returned to the land. Among the rest, strikes and disorders became common. The Mensheviks regained their influence.

At the Tenth Party Congress in March 1921 Zinoviev declared that if a congress of workers (proposed by Shlyapnikov) were called, ninety-nine per cent of it would be Menshevik, Social Revolutionary, and in general non-Communist. Trotsky attacked this as a great exaggeration, but admitted that in any free workers' elections, non-Communists would be heavily represented. He added that the Party was "in duty bound to retain its dictatorship, regardless of the temporary vacillations of the amorphous masses, regardless of the temporary vacillations of the working class."

As early as 1919 Lenin himself had found it necessary to make a remark crucial to the whole Leninist attitude to the working class: "We recognize neither freedom, nor equality, *nor labour democracy* [my italics] if they are opposed to the interests of the emancipation of labour from the oppression of capital." In 1920 he was insisting that "revolutionary violence" was essential "against the faltering and unrestrained elements of the toiling masses themselves."

For the Bolshevik policies had proved economically disastrous and their methods of enforcement politically detested by all classes. Even within the Party itself worker groupings were organizing against the dictatorship. March 1921 saw the crux. As late as March 8, Lenin was still insisting to the Tenth Congress that the abandonment of grain requisitioning in favor of free trade "would still unfailingly lead to the rule of the White Guard, to the triumph of capitalism, to complete restoration of the old regime. And I repeat: we must clearly recognise this political danger."

But the Bolsheviks were at the end of their tether. On March 2, the workers and sailors of the Kronstadt naval base had set up a Revolutionary Committee, and as Lenin spoke a major battle was raging which was to end only on March 18. Though labeled counter-revolutionary, the rebellion had mass support even among the local Communists. Lenin admitted privately, "They do not want the White Guards and they do not want our power either."

Kronstadt, in fact, marked the break. It was war on the *idea* of libertarian radical socialism, on proletarian democracy. On the other side there remained only the idea of the Party. Lenin's party, cut off from its social justification, now rested on dogma alone. He assumed that popular, or proletarian, support could be dispensed with and that mere integrity of motive would be adequate, would justify everything in the long run.

With even the proletariat so strongly disaffected, Lenin admitted that "we have failed to convince the broad masses." Policies which led to peasant revolt capped by proletarian revolt could only lead to the eventual collapse of the regime. As so often before, Lenin—a week later—suddenly changed his mind just in time and insisted (against much doctrinaire resistance in the Party) on the New Economic Policy. War Communism was abandoned. The struggle against the peasantry was called off. Taxation and a measure of free trade were substituted for forced procurement of grain.

The question now remained whether to relax politically as well as economically. Lenin took the view that (as in 1912) the Party was in so difficult a position politically that the utmost discipline, more than in the Revolution or the Civil War, was required. On the last day of the Tenth Congress he suddenly produced two new resolutions. The second condemned the view that the trade unions should have any controlling role in industry as non-Marxist and "therefore inconsistent with membership of the Party," since "Marxism teaches us that only the political party of the working class, i.e., the Communist Party, is capable of uniting, educating and organizing such a vanguard of the proletariat and of the working masses as is capable of resisting the inevitable petty-bourgeois waverings of these masses . . . [and] their trade union prejudices." This was, of course, a reassertion of essential Leninism as it had been since *What Is to Be Done?* The first resolution, on Party unity, called for the immediate dissolution of all groups within the Party with "platforms." This was in effect to ban the factions arguing for inner-Party democracy and for workers' control—and to destroy forever the old Party liberties.

The political problem in the country as a whole was similar. The change to NEP and the abandonment of crash socialization amounted to admission that the already much revived Mensheviks had been right all along.

The choice was reasonably straightforward. Either the dictatorship must be tightened up, the other socialist parties finally suppressed, and critics within the Communist Party itself silenced, or there must be a reconciliation with the Mensheviks and the Social Revolutionaries, and a general acceptance of the views of the democratic and worker factions in the Communist Party. This course held the promise of reconciliation with the people and a broad socialist and democratic program economically not much different from that practiced in 1921–1929, but far easier in terms of political and popular tension.

As Leonard Schapiro has commented, "In 1921 the fate of the country lay in the hands of Lenin. He had a chance of burying past enmities and of carrying the vast majority of the country with him in an attempt to build up ruined Russia on the basis of co-operation and legal order, and not of the dictatorship of an unpopular minority." George Orwell remarks that Lenin "is one of those politicians who win an undeserved reputation by dying prematurely." But if he had died or been incapacitated in 1920, more prematurely still, it could not be said that he had missed his last and greatest opportunity.

Lenin's choice was the immediate total suppression of the Mensheviks and Social Revolutionaries.

At the Tenth Party Conference, in May 1921, Karl Radek, with rather more frankness than Lenin, dotted the i's by explaining that if the Mensheviks were left at liberty, now that the Communists had adopted their policy, they would demand political power, while to concede freedom to the Social Revolutionaries when the "enormous mass" of the peasants was opposed to the Communists would be suicide. So the Menshevik Party was finally crushed. The Social Revolutionaries followed, receiving the death blow at a show trial of their leaders in 1922. (Soviet representatives had promised the Second International that there would be no death sentences, much to Lenin's rage.)

Lenin's attitude to the Menshevik leader Martov, almost alone among his opponents, was not simply cold hostility. In fact, it is often cited to show Lenin's human feelings, especially in contrast to such men as Stalin. There is some truth in this. And Soviet journals have lately officially condemned an author who suggested that Lenin had called for a blind eye to be turned to Martov's departure from Russia in 1920. An often told story is that when Lenin was dying he asked Krupskaya, "They say Martov is dying too. Is it true?" Martov, though remaining a convinced Menshevik, had loyally supported the Soviet regime throughout the Civil War. At any rate, no serious attempt seems to have been made to prevent him and certain other Mensheviks (partly as the result of a hunger strike in prison) from leaving the country in 1920. Clearly, a decision had been taken on the elimination of the Mensheviks without recourse to public trial, or any of the extreme measures to be inflicted on the Social Revolutionaries. But in 1921, when the pressure was being intensified, two of Martov's brothers, his sister, his two cousins, and his sixteen-year-old nephew were arrested, together with the bulk of the leading Menshevik survivors. Recently published letters of Lenin's written in 1922 contain what can only be called frenzied calls for further repressions against the Mensheviks. Georgi Chicherin, the Commissar for Foreign Affairs, had apparently pleaded for moderation, and was called a "lunatic" by Lenin for this. Lenin urged special measures against counterrevolutionary writers and teachers, and one of his last letters is a severe criticism of the Politburo for too lenient treatment of the former Menshevik historian Rozhkov.

Politically speaking, the elimination of opposition and of indiscipline meant that Lenin had at last created the thoroughly centralized party, and the one-party state, which had been implicit in all his writings since the beginning of the century.

One major task remained—the extension of the same system to the rest of the world.

The time when Lenin had trusted the Western socialists, and in particular the German Social Democrats, to create socialism was long past: even the then left-wing leader was now "the renegade Kautsky." Moreover, the expected revolutionizing of the Western masses had not taken place. Only—briefly and precariously—in Hungary did a Communist regime come to power.

Lenin had argued against Kautsky in 1918 that "to count on a European revolution is obligatory for a Marxist if a revolutionary situation is at hand," as he maintained it was. Then in November, when the imperial regime was overthrown in Germany, Lenin had claimed:

> A whole group of countries is seized with the flame of the workers' revolution. In this respect our efforts and the sacrifices that we have made have been justified. They have turned out to be not an adventure, as claimed by the slander of our enemy, but a necessary transition to the international revolution, through which a country must pass which has been placed in a position of leadership in spite of its undeveloped and backward state.

But even in defeated and ruined Germany, where the sole important non-Russian Communist group—Rosa Luxemburg's Spartakusbund—worked for a Soviet republic, the masses remained attached to the old Social Democrats. It seems that for the remainder of his life Lenin was never quite able to believe this, continuing to imagine that Germany was on the verge of communism. Nor, for a Marxist, is it easily explainable how socialist leaders could betray the workers and yet retain their confidence.

Moreover, the German Social Democrats of that period were no Mensheviks, but men experienced in politics as well as closely linked with the workers. When it came to the crisis they preferred democracy to communism, and proved able to maneuver between, and to crush in detail, both their Kornilovs and their Lenins.

It was not even the case that Rosa Luxemburg and her German Communists wholly approved of Lenin. She wrote most critically of his suppression of democracy, and when Lenin now started negotiations for a new Communist International to replace the "bankrupt" Second International, she strongly opposed the move.

In our own times it is often forgotten that in the revolutionary movement Red Rosa still enjoyed a greater reputation than Lenin himself. His current prominence was due to the fact that he alone had so far seized power; but in those revolutionary years this was widely thought of as a temporary advantage. The possibility of his fall was very apparent and menacing. And, on the other hand, many expected a German revolution which would add to Rosa Luxemburg's general repute the physical advantages temporarily denied her.

Her murder in January 1919, after she had taken part in an insurrection she knew to be premature, did not in principle change the German Communist viewpoint. on the new International. When Lenin summoned a group of foreign Communists to Moscow in March, the German delegate continued to oppose the idea of a Comintern, was assured that it had been dropped, and suddenly had it sprung on him at a meeting of alleged foreign delegates, almost all of whom were actually in Soviet employ. He now just abstained.

With the Comintern in being at Lenin's insistence, the German Communist Party finally acceded to it. But for a couple of years it remained a congeries of disparate left-wing sects, many of whom were repeating the various errors which Lenin had, with the greatest difficulty, eradicated among the Bolsheviks.

Meanwhile, in 1920, he made another type of attempt to further the European revolution when he launched the Red Army "to test Poland with bayonets," against the almost unanimous advice of Polish Bolsheviks. The delegates of the Second Congress of the Comintern saw on huge wall maps in their meeting hall the daily advance of the Red Army which, it was hoped, would open Europe to communism.

But Lenin's old rival Joseph Pilsudski, whose brother had been a fellow conspirator of Alexander Ulyanov's in 1887, and of whose Polish socialist followers' militant activity in 1905 Lenin had written enviously, now defeated him at Warsaw; and within weeks the expansionist élan of Russian Bolshevism was at an end for twenty years. Further attempts to revolutionize Germany and other European states were equally futile. Failure, as ever, led to greater emphasis on discipline and consolidation.

The new International had attracted a hotchpotch of odd socialist left-wing factions, most of them bearing little resemblance to the Bolshevik Party. Nor was there at first any rigorous insistence on Leninist organizational principles. Even the Norwegian Labor Party was able to join the new body. The final step, the decision that the totality of Leninist organizational principles should apply in the advanced countries, had yet to be taken.

But now in 1920 Lenin imposed the famous Twenty-One Conditions. In effect, these meant that every Communist Party throughout the world should be a carbon copy of the Russian one; and that each Party should come under the direct control of the Comintern sitting in Moscow. Theoretically, this did not give the Russians control over the other parties. On paper, their own Party too had to submit to overriding Comintern authority. In practice, however, the Russian view was invariably decisive. And over the years, the whole organization was always under effective Soviet control.

In 1920, to guide the International, Lenin also produced the last of his effective works, *Left-Wing Communism: an Infantile Disorder*. It was concerned to condemn those newly hatched Communists outside the Soviet Union who were always refusing compromises of various sorts on principle rather than as a matter of tactics. It was the same problem he had had with Bukharin and the "Left" in 1918.

The Communists of the West were now instructed to judge solely by expediency and the struggle for power—the only difficulty was to be that their judgment was almost invariably wrong, so that the new "scientific" Leninist attempts at revolution in Germany and elsewhere in the early twenties were no less disastrous than those which had been undertaken in a thoughtless and romantic style. The constant belief that a revolutionary situation existed where this was clearly a complete misconception is a striking reflection on the failure in Marxist analysis of Lenin's disciples, at any rate outside Russia itself.

Moreover, as in Russia, an important section of the revolutionary left throughout the world was not merely detached from the movement but set against it. The Communist parties were taught to regard all other forms of socialist principle and organization as heretical, hostile, and treacherous. Stalin is always, and rightly, held in part to blame for the disruption of the German left in the face of the rise of Nazism in the early thirties, by his insistence that Social Democracy was the main enemy. Lenin seems to bear a similar responsibility for the rise of Italian Fascism a decade earlier. He equally disrupted the Italian left. In fact, his attacks were directed not merely at the equivalent of the Social Democrats but even more at genuine revolutionaries like Serrati, whose fault was simply that he did not accept the Bolshevik model *in toto*.

The imposition of the "democratic centralist" party system to apply all over the world is perhaps Lenin's most remarkable decision. It reflected the feeling that the old Marxist idea of the revolutionary development of the proletariat was not to be trusted, even in the advanced countries, and needed to be replaced by subjectivist will power. More profoundly, in fact, it amounted to the extension of Lenin's own political personality on a world scale. The personal drama played out in Russia, in which it had gradually become apparent that he himself was the only mind and force which could be trusted, was now extended universally to the international scene.

The question (which we consider in the next chapter) of how far Lenin was beginning to rethink his position in the last years of his life applies also to the international field. In his very last speech, in November 1922 (to the Fourth Congress of the Comintern), while he was generally encouraging, at the very end he remarked in a somewhat incoherent passage, that the approach of the member parties was "too Russian" and that this was "a great mistake." But there is no real sign that he was intending to retract the "Bolshevizing" principles of organization and ideology which had meanwhile been imposed on the foreign parties.

Lenin's Afterthoughts

IX

On May 26, 1922, Lenin had his first stroke, and
henceforth, except for a short period at the end
of the year, he could no longer take an active
part in politics. Cut off from the immediacies of
political life, he gave his attention to the unex-
pected defects that afflicted his revolution. As
we have seen, he had already noted that there
had been a failure "to convince the broad
masses." He had spoken of the "adventurers and
rogues," the "boastful and noisy elements," the
"careerists" who had flocked into the Party. He
had noted many bureaucratic "deformities" in
the Soviet state. He had referred to "that same
Russian apparatus borrowed from Tsarism and
simply covered with a Soviet veneer." On the
eve of his stroke, he had condemned the prev-
alence of "personal spite and malice" in Party
committees.

On his recovery from this first stroke, he

criticized "the sea of illegality" in which the country was living. He attacked the parasitism and carelessness of those in authority and gave special words for Communist boasts and lies, "com-boasts" and "com-lies." More fundamentally, he noted that "the Communist kernel lacks general culture" and said that although the culture of the bourgeoisie in Russia was "wretched," it was in any case greater than that of "the responsible Communists." In his very last articles, he attacked "bureaucratic misrule and wilfulness," spoke of the condition of the state as "repugnant," and concluded gloomily that "we lack sufficient civilization to enable us to pass straight on to Socialism, although we have the political requisites."

That is, he was to some extent belatedly recognizing the validity of Marx's own conditions for revolution— an experienced and educated proletariat with an adequately developed "culture" and "civilization."

Nor were the "political requisites" as satisfactory as implied. It is true that he had them in the sense that his Party enjoyed the exercise of sole power. But the Party itself was exhibiting grave misbehavior. He found that the Georgian Communists, whom he had rather reluctantly imposed by arms on an almost unanimously hostile Georgia, were being bullied, even physically maltreated, by Stalin, Ordzhonikidze, and others. Within the leadership he saw feuds which to him represented a real danger to the state.

The Lenin of these last years, Grigori Pyatakov remarked in 1928, was not "the real Lenin," not the man who "had had the courage to make a proletarian revolution first, and then to set about creating the objective conditions theoretically necessary as a preliminary to such a revolution. What was the October Revolution, what indeed is the Communist Party, but a miracle?" The Party's basic principle, Pyatakov added, was the achievement of otherwise unattainable social ends by "boundless coercion."

All the same, he was clearly *a* real Lenin. And it is the first time any feeling is given that if he had survived and recovered, he might have sought a more profound solution to Russia's difficulties than any that he had so far provided. Perhaps he would have found that the maintenance of the miracle required higher powers of political levitation than Russia, or the Communist Party, possessed. It would be unfair to suggest that Lenin was inherently incapable of the larger effort.

Unfair, but not grossly unfair. He had changed, but he had not yet shown any signs whatever of questioning the one-party state and the democratic-centralist party. He was shaken by the symptoms of mindless despotism and intellectual decay, but he did not see them as the natural, let alone the inevitable, products of that state and that Party. His solution for the factional strife among the leaders was (in December 1922) the futile one of recommending an increase in the size of the Central Committee.

On March 9, 1923, he had a final stroke which wholly incapacitated him from further political activity. He died on January 21, 1924.

The Heritage

Any judgment of Lenin faces us with the most basic questions of political ethics. Those who judge by purity of intention will, or may, tend to a more favorable conclusion than those who judge by the fruits.

His career may be looked upon as a brilliant success in which, against all the odds, he imposed his conceptions on a vast country and created a method and a mechanism which, despite occasional distortions, is still working to impose those conceptions on the entire world. Others would sum him up as a narrow doctrinaire who through a series of odd chances managed to seize power in a backward area and in doing so created a state quite incompatible with his original purpose. The two views do not necessarily contradict one another.

The development of Leninism, and of the post-Leninist Marxisms which go even further along the road in substituting revolutionary will power for objective social circumstances, is to some extent confused by one obvious fact. Marx, while laying down the objective conditions necessary for a socialist revolution, does not omit to add the "subjective" element of proletarian political organization, consciously advancing the historical process. Lenin, in one view, might be thought to be merely putting greater emphasis on the subjective element. At the same time, he at least asserted that objective conditions too in Russia had ripened to a degree which made proletarian revolution legitimate. But in the first place, Lenin's extra emphasis on the subjective is not a minor matter, but a big shift. And secondly, his claim that objective circumstances all the same gave his revolution an adequate Marxist basis is very shaky. Indeed, he saw this himself and, as we have seen, at first justified the seizure of power as merely the priority chance had given briefly and temporarily to a backward element in what would soon be a European or a world revolution, in which the advanced industrial countries would preponderate— with the revolutionary capital being moved, as Lenin put it, to Berlin or London.

Lenin left a system of party organization which has been imitated round the world—and not only on the left. And he provided for its guidance a theory of extreme tactical flexibility. It is true that the centralized party and the tactics of pure expediency have proved efficacious only in the hands of a very small number of individual leaders—in particular, Mao Tse-tung and, in another sense, Stalin. The Leninists who have created or consolidated their own one-party states have been— almost as much as Lenin himself—individual pioneers.

For the trouble about his works seen as instructions in revolutionary tactics is that no criterion is laid down about what is a legitimate tactical compromise and what is "opportunism." It depends on the circumstances—that is, on the balance of class and other forces. But no method of estimating these is given: it is simply a matter of sound judgment. And his tactical writings are on the whole either so general as to be of no great value to the revolutionary or so particular as to go little further than analyzing specific Russian situations at one time or another.

It is in the interest of those who have succeeded, or inherited a success, to imply that the success was inevitable. In reality, one is struck time and time again by the element of accident in the whole story of the Revolution. From the Tsarevich's hemophilia and the intervention of Rasputin to the inaccuracy of Fanny Kaplan's shooting, time and time again key events are "meerly accidental, whatever the pompous history in 8vo sayes," as John Aubrey puts it in his *Brief Lives*.

More generally, it is nothing against Lenin to say that his achievements could not have taken place except, first, by accidents of history which even he himself did not expect; and second, in the particular political culture in which he found himself. It is difficult to accept the historicism which, while on the one hand interpreting history in terms of the vast movement of social forces, at the same time sees in crucial individuals something like the natural incarnations demanded by and produced by the circumstances.

And if personality played its part, the same should be said of the absence of an adequate personality among his competitors. There were, it is true, men like Savinkov and Tseretelli, who saw things clearly—but they lacked (through no historical or psychological fatality that one can see) the ability to dominate their colleagues. Men like Kornilov had determination, but no political sense.

If Lenin had lived to the age of various political leaders, revolutionary and otherwise, of our time—Mao Tse-tung, Churchill, Tito, de Gaulle, Adenauer, for example—he might still have ruled Russia in the late 1930s or early 1940s. (Mao, born in 1893, was finally victorious in *his* civil war in 1949, at the age of fifty-six—and is alive as I write in 1971, more than twenty years later. Lenin was only fifty when he won his civil war in 1920 and dead at the age of fifty-three.) Those who hold that Lenin's survival after 1924 would have radically changed the course of events in Russia must also regard his early death as a decisive accident, historically speaking.

One point on which all would presumably agree is that he himself was a successful political tactician, and in a far more profound sense than such a description might ordinarily imply. For he first planned, and then created, the new model party which was the tactical instrument of his triumphs. Nor were these triumphs with the range of ordinary politics. He "Cast the kingdoms old / Into another mould."

The Leninist would, of course, make greater claims than this—that Lenin mastered and fulfilled the laws of history; that he made a proletarian revolution (in Georg Lukács' words, that he was the class-consciousness of the proletariat in visible form); that he laid the foundations of a new, world-embracing order.

But the ability to seize power and to replace a ruling class or elite by a new one is not in itself any guarantee of the possession of a satisfactory general theory of history, or of the capacity to create a superior, let alone supreme, form of human society.

In general, it might be granted that in several ways things have not gone as he foresaw. Above all, the "capitalist" system which he believed to be on the point of collapse has survived. This can hardly be taken otherwise than implying that Marxism (or rather classical Marxism plus Lenin's amendments to it) was not a true description of the world: or, to put it at its most charitable, if in any sense true, not true enough.

Secondly, while the system in present-day Russia has a good claim to be the inheritor and extension of that which Lenin set up in the early 1920s, it has at any rate

not developed much in the direction of the great extension of liberty, creativity, and so forth, which Lenin
foresaw as coming into flower quite soon after revolutionary victory, and which, even allowing for an—
occasionally admitted—prematureness in seizing power,
should at any rate have shown at least some signs of
life when a vast new Russian proletariat had established
itself—let us say, some time in the last thirty-odd years.

Lenin's comment, in his last phase, that what was
lacking in Soviet Russia was sufficient "culture" to
attain socialism, that the mere "political requisites"
were not sufficient, seems a faint adumbration of an
empirical, non-"systematic" view of the problem. We
have suggested (page 8), the importance of this lack
of any true political, or civic culture in Russia.[1]

We are bound to be judging Lenin and Leninism,
and indeed Russia in general, to some extent at least
from the point of view of our own society and its history. It should be asserted firmly that Britain and the
United States are and were (as Lenin himself, of course,
fully recognized) far more developed politically and so-
cially than Russia. It has been argued that Russia's
comparative primitiveness could be and was turned into
advantage, enabling the country to bypass parts of the
historical process. The observer in London is, in any

---

[1] Since the above was penned, Mr. K. S. Karol, in a most
penetrating article in the *New Statesman* (January 1, 1971)
has quoted a Soviet official as remarking to him, "Our
country has no civil tradition. The taste for association, for
organizing communal life together, for getting to know each
other and taking decisions together, never really existed in
Russia. Between the czar and the mujik there was nothing;
equally between one mujik and another there was nothing
except for essential personal relationships. We were and
we remain a huge body, colossal even, but shapeless and
deprived of articulation, of that political fabric on which
the modern states of Europe were built. The Revolution
failed to make the Russian masses articulate because the
experiments of Lenin's soviets were quickly stifled. . . ."

case, set in an accumulation of historical, political, and other experience: and he may thus be in a position to make certain criticisms and suggest why certain options open in the West failed to emerge, or failed to emerge far enough, in Russia at that time.

The absence of such experience or tradition had meant that the country's revolutionary intelligentsia, including Lenin, had no political equipment for the post-revolutionary period except for what they could derive from abstract theory. In Lenin's pre-revolutionary works there is no sign of awareness of the fact that in *any* political regime there are certain precautions to be taken, certain rules to be observed—and certain lessons to be learned from the politics of the past. In his post-revolutionary writings the problems of real politics, and the corruption of power and the establishment of interests, come to him as a constant shock to which he can only suggest piecemeal and (as it turned out) useless remedies.

Nor was Marx of much help. When Milovan Djilas points out that the defect of Marxism was the absence of a theory of political liberty, he is putting his finger on a very important crux, and not only from a libertarian point of view. For what in fact emerges is that Marx's notion of post-revolutionary politics is entirely schematic. A Social Democratic party, representing the working class, will rule a given country democratically as a proletarian dictatorship. Though Marx had seen and recognized that, in bourgeois state forms, political machines and individual leaders had been able to set themselves up even to a large degree against the main bourgeois class interest, it does not seem to have occurred to him to consider the real possibilities of a socialist state.

The anarchist Bakunin, whatever his weaknesses, had his finger on this great flaw in the Marxist case when he said, "Those previous workers having just become rulers or representatives of the people will cease being workers; they will look at the workers from their heights, they will represent not the people but themselves. . . . He who doubts it does not know human nature."

In all this, Lenin followed Marx. The actual history of the Soviet state seems to teach that this was a disastrous omission. And, moreover, it was one which could easily have been remedied by a little attention to the political thinkers of the past. One reason why the American Revolution did not produce a dictatorship was clearly that the founding fathers had observed the lessons of history in this field. The works of Jefferson, of Richard Henry Lee, the Federalist Papers, are all replete with warnings against ambition and demagogy and, more important, on ways of controlling them, of checks and balances.

Nor is it a matter of "bourgeois" and "proletarian." The English and American revolutions of 1688 and 1776 are in contrast with the French and the Russian revolutions of 1789 and 1917. The organizers of the first two had much civic experience; those of the last two had little, or none.

It is not even so much that the Anglo-Saxon experience was one of "democracy" as that it has taken place in societies based on the conflict of different interests and possessing mechanisms to reconcile them as undestructively as possible, as against societies without such checks and balances. For example, the Rome of the fourth century B.C. had such institutions, so that even the incredibly bitter and long-drawn-out struggles over the Licinian Laws, which in any Greek city would have caused the streets to run with blood, were in the end settled constitutionally. It is, in effect, a matter less of general principle than of political mechanics: in cybernetic terms, the British system has "negative feedback" while Russia did and does not, so that the latter can easily lapse into excesses of despotism and massacre and cannot so easily be brought back to normal.

In fact Lenin had no *political* philosophy covering a post-revolutionary period, no notion that a proletarian democracy might require any system of sanctions to control its representatives. The gap was filled by authoritarian expediency.

The system of one-party dictatorship and rigorous intra-Party discipline now imposed, could only, it may be thought, have led to something at least resembling Stalinism. Even when things had been a good deal less strict, in 1918, Rosa Luxemburg had deduced an inevitable degeneration, mainly on the grounds that the absence of political liberty and of freedom of debate must lead to the debasement of the intellectual and moral faculties of the leadership. She wrote in a famous passage:

Freedom only for the supporters of the Government, only for the members of one Party—however numerous they may be—is no freedom at all. Freedom is always and exclusively freedom for the one who thinks differently. Not because of any fanatical concept of "justice" but because all that is instructive, wholesome and purifying in political freedom depends on this essential characteristic, and its effectiveness vanishes when "freedom" becomes a special privilege. . . .

Without general elections, without unrestricted freedom of Press and assembly, without a free struggle of opinion, life dies out in every public institution, becomes a mere semblance of life in which only the bureaucracy remains as the new active element. Public life gradually falls asleep, a few dozen party leaders of inexhaustible energy and boundless experience direct and rule. Among them, in reality only a dozen oustanding heads do the leading, and an élite of the working class is invited from time to time to meetings where they are to applaud the speeches of the leaders. . . . Yes, we can go even further: such conditions must inevitably cause a brutalization of public life: attempted assassinations, shooting of hostages, etc.

It may, of course, be argued that Rosa Luxemburg was wrong, in the sense that no such revolution as she envisaged was possible. And it is certainly true that the mass, democratic, proletarian access to power foreshadowed by classical Marxism has nowhere achieved reality. In Russia, in particular, there seems in any case to have been little possibility of such a development, whether we take the Marxist or any other point of view. It can thus be held (as Alasdair MacIntyre puts it) that the only "Marxist" revolution possible in Russia was that which Lenin actually effected. Rosa Luxemburg's reply was, in effect, that unless Lenin's revolution rapidly abandoned the bureaucratic and authoritarian structure, arguably inevitable at the start, it would cease in any meaningful sense to be describable as a proletarian revolution within the Marxist framework.

In fact, critics of Lenin are entitled to say that in the long run his principle of the centralized party and its "vanguard" role meant that his revolution could no longer be described in the Marxist categories, and amounted to substituting for the old regime the rule not of the working class but of a political and bureaucratic elite.

In spite of his constant complaints about bureaucracy in his last years, no such possibility seems seriously to have entered his head. The Bolshevik grip on power was, he seems to have thought, the only and necessary precondition for realizing his more general ideas. With this once accepted, the complete alienation of the proletariat could be interpreted as a proletarian dictatorship, the tighter and increasingly autocratic centralism as a higher form of democracy.

The Bolshevik power, in fact, justified everything. It may be urged (and this is no mere debating point, since it was quite clearly the verdict of the masses who underwent the experience) that Lenin's promise of "Peace, Bread, Land" resulted in Civil War, Famine, and (after a decade of precarious tenure) Collectivization. The death roll in the Imperialist War, about which he had been so eloquently condemnatory, was greatly exceeded by the deaths in Russia from 1918 to 1922. He got Russia out of the war less than a year earlier than the date it in any case ended. The Civil War which resulted went on till 1920. Russia's dead in 1914–1917 were less than two million. If she had held on for another year, and even suffered another million killed, that would have been far and away less than the death roll actually produced which cannot, on Soviet statistics, have been much less than fourteen million.

Lenin would doubtless (except as a matter of propaganda at the time) have accepted the casualties as a price no doubt unfortunate, but after all worth paying for the success of the Revolution. When we turn to the longer-term results we are on more substantial ground.

The question whether the Stalin regime in Russia (and its current successor) was a natural sequel to Lenin's, or whether it was a gross, unforeseeable, and disastrous perversion of his legacy has, of course, been widely debated.

Perhaps the most crucial moment when fetishism of the Party and of "democratic centralism" played a decisive role was in 1930. Stalin's first crash collectivization program had met with disaster. All over the country, the Party members, and still more the people, spoke up for the assumption of power by Bukharin and the "Rightist" faction. In the Planning Commission, the economic Commissariats, and the intelligentsia in general, once again the possibility of a united socialist government was much discussed.

Under any other system, it would have been the time for the Rightist leaders to stand forward. Their warnings had proved correct. But they made no effort to achieve power. Bukharin and Rykov and the others explicitly condemned any question of standing against "the Party"—that is, against the Congresses and Central Committees which Stalin's Secretariat had packed.

As for the question of a united front with other socialist forces, they rejected such an idea with horror, precisely on Leninist principles.

As a result, Stalin's policy defeat was accompanied by a complete political victory and by the end of 1930 he had removed the last non-Stalinist from the Politburo.

It also seems likely that when crisis loomed, the strict one-party system would have broken down but for the emergence of a man who at least shared with Lenin an immense will power and a complete certainty as to the rightness of his own conclusions: it was one of his Trotskyite enemies who said of Stalin in the early thirties, "If it were not for that so-and-so . . . everything would have fallen to pieces by now."

Only believers in historical inevitability would argue that Stalin was inevitable, that he was simply and solely Lenin's heir. But it is at least clear that no very liberal character could have come to lead the Party, that as a result of the way in which Lenin left *the party* organized it was likely to fall into the hands of the best manipulator of the apparatus. Even Trotsky, who had abandoned his early criticism of democratic centralism in 1917, finally came round to admitting that "It is rather tempting to draw the inference that future Stalinism was already rooted in Bolshevik centralism or, more sweepingly, in the underground hierarchy of professional revolutionaries."

At any rate, one must say that it is what actually happened to the Soviet regime and to the Soviet Communist Party. When we consider post-Leninist Russia we are, as Professor MacIntyre remarks, in the position of judging Lenin (as we are in judging any other historical figure) in the light of hindsight, with knowledge of the results of his actions which he could not possess at the time. Even our hindsight, however, is much cluttered up with myth. There are many widespread notions about the past which have, as it were, entered the public consciousness without adequate verification. One of these in effect excuses the barbarities of the Stalin regime by referring to those of Tsarism, allegedly as bad or worse.

It needs to be strongly emphasized that this is by no means the case. Up to 1905, the Tsarist regime was in the most literal sense an autocracy, and even after that date it was the most backward polity in Europe. Nevertheless it was progressing. And, even more important, it had never produced anything remotely comparable to the terror of the Communist regime.

For example, from the 1860s till about 1902 the death sentences amounted to no more (for 30 assassinations, including that of Tsar Alexander II) than a few score. A confidential Tsarist document gives 48 executions, while a Soviet source (*Small Soviet Encyclopedia*, first edition) gives 94, from 1866 to 1900.

After the 1905 Revolution, political assassinations became widespread, causing about 1400 deaths in 1906 and 3000 in 1907. Large areas were put under special regulations, and courts-martial tried those accused of terrorism and rebellion. These courts existed only for a few months, but over a thousand executions resulted. The highest figure that can be arrived at from Soviet sources for the whole pre-revolutionary period is about 14,000.

Generally speaking, if we set a limit of 25,000 for all executions, pogrom murders, and deaths in prison of the period from 1866 to 1917, it will be an absolute maximum. The total maximum imprisoned (in 1912) was 183,949. It is absurd to compare these figures with those of the Soviet epoch, let alone justify the latter by them. Over the first half-century of Soviet rule, the executions were at least fifty times as numerous as over the last half-century of Tsarist rule, and the maximum number of prisoners at least seventy times as great. Moreover, in every other respect as well, the standards of humanitarianism had enormously worsened. In Tsarist times, torture was the rarest and most scandalous exception, and the hostage system quite unknown. Lenin himself, the most intransigent enemy of the Tsarist regime, had suffered exile in a village where he was free to work, received letters, got an allowance, met his friends, hunted, and so on. In the later period, any friend of a friend of some maker of a minor joke about the government was locked in a camp and working himself to death on starvation rations, without hope of release. And the Tsarist victims, unlike those of Stalin, were at least genuine rebels or assassins.

Equally, among both those who approve and those who disapprove in general of the Soviet regime there is a largely mythical notion that it has made industrial and social advances which would not have been produced by any other methods. In fact, the industrialization of Russia at various times in the last half-century of Tsardom was proceeding as fast as (and in some respects faster than) it did in the post-revolutionary period. (It has been said that an economist in 1914, given a view of the present world, would be surprised only by the industrial development of Singapore, Formosa, and Hong Kong and by the decay of Russian agriculture.) It is certainly true that a different style of recent political rule in Russia must have affected the balance and content of industry. An aggressively nationalist, right-wing regime would no doubt have placed something of the same emphasis on the heavy and war industries, and a liberal democracy a good deal less.

Clearly, a vast constructive effort has been put in. But, on the other hand, the negative economic effects resulting directly from the political system have been comparably enormous, starting with the destruction or emigration of a large segment of Russia's skill in the time of the Revolution and going through the decimation—or, rather, considerably more than decimation—of the newly trained industrial and economic cadres in the thirties, together with the enormous wastages of the various crash programs which have marked the whole period.

Again, it is sometimes thought that the vast increase in the educational system is a product of the Revolution. In fact, the educational plans already approved before World War I would have had about the same result, eliminating illiteracy by about 1930—and in fact it was largely this prewar plan which the Soviet government actually put into effect. The one area in which major and as then unforeseen improvements have been made is in the medical and other social services. These are now found in most industrial countries, and it is hard to imagine that they depend upon any specific political system. But even in 1914 a comprehensive system of industrial insurance for employees was already in existence in Russia.

It seems clear that the sacrifices of Lenin's and of Stalin's rule—running into tens of millions of deaths, and other moral and physical suffering on a vast scale —could be justified only if they had produced a society incomparably superior to anything in the Russian past, anything in the reformist West. Few would now argue that this has occurred.

Now, either the Stalin regime and the present situation in Russia are the legitimate results of Lenin's actions; in which case he can be judged accordingly. Or they are illegitimate, unforeseen; in which case he must surely be taken to have submitted the country to great suffering in the name of a theory which has proved, after all, defective in mastering and predicting events. Either way, a judgment of the present-day U.S.S.R. is clearly the crux. If we accept it as a reasonably Good Society, Lenin is vindicated. If we find its condition largely deplorable, the verdict must be much harsher.

Perspectives

XI

The official attitude to Lenin in the U.S.S.R. is, and has long been, to make him the object of an extraordinary cult. Pronouncements in the most varied fields are justified far less by arguments on their merits than on their congruence with texts from his *Works*—sometimes, as we shall see, employed with inadequate discretion. Terms like "blasphemy" are freely used of those who speak critically of him. The solemn announcement by a delegate to the Twenty-second Party Congress that he had appeared to her in a dream to complain of sharing Stalin's tomb was received with the utmost solemnity by her fellows. (Though we must, indeed, concede that it was a British Leninist, the late Professor J. B. S. Haldane, who made public the lesser miracle that reading Lenin had cured his stomach ulcers.)

In 1970, the centenary of his birth was celebrated on a vast scale in the Soviet Union. There was a huge output of novels, stories, essays, plays, pictorial albums, symphonies, poems, films, and so on about him. About a third of the daily output of press, theater, and cinema in April 1970 was devoted to him. Some of this seemed excessive even to official critics: for example, stories showing Lenin's common touch which spoke of his skill in wielding the scythe—something he never did at all. Chocolate cakes with his name on top, raffles of Lenin busts, theme songs dedicated to his memory were also criticized. There was an objection, too, to a story for children which represented him as kissing his wife's hair. On the other hand, one or two realists were also censured for mentioning, for example, Lenin removing his bowler hat and mopping his bald head with a handkerchief.

The general impression was that the whole thing was greatly overdone, and boredom was induced on a vast scale. Miss Natalia Makarova, the prima ballerina who "defected" to the West during that year, tells us that it was clear that the leadership had even contrived to bore *themselves* over the matter.

The merely mechanical nature of "Leninist" ideology in the Soviet Union was well illustrated in the theses put out for the centenary by the Central Committee of the Party. This huge document, taking up two and a half closely printed pages of *Pravda*, named five criteria Lenin had supposedly put forward, by which the Communist movement in Western Europe could be judged. It turned out that these were not Lenin's at all. On the contrary, they were criteria put forward by the Austrian Social Democrat Otto Bauer in his *Bolshevism or Social Democracy* on the ripeness of a working-class movement worthy of taking power (and interesting beyond the present context as a declaration of classical Marxism). The tests were: the degree of organization, numbers, the role of the working class in the process of production and distribution, activity, and education. It was precisely the lack of these, Bauer pointed out, that made it certain that the Russian Communists could not produce or run a workers' state. These theses were in fact violently *attacked* by Lenin.

The explanation seems to be that some Soviet expert found them jotted down by Lenin in notes he made on the tasks of the Comintern in July 1920. The real point is, however, that no one reading them noticed anything wrong until they were finally detected by (apparently) Walter Ulbricht. That is, ideas specifically rejected by Lenin sounded all right to "Leninists" so long as they thought he had said them.

For all this rather mechanical piety, to the extent that the Soviet Communist Party is still organized on "democratic centralist" principles and the Soviet state is still conceived of as machinery for driving the masses in the required political direction, it is recognizably Leninist. The only fundamental question that arises is whether Lenin would have felt that a system of tutelage over the masses would be required after half a century of Communist rule—indeed, would be *more* centralized, *less* subject to debate than at the beginning; and whether he might not have noted a decline in Soviet standards of political intelligence, and a vast increase in those bureaucratic tendencies against which he warned, but which even at the time he found impossible to halt.

But, apart from official Kremlin ideology, there are, of course, many different trains of thought now in existence which appeal to Lenin for their authority, each of them condemning the others. For Mao, Castro, and Tito, for the Dubcek leadership in Prague as much as for the Politburo in Moscow which ejected it by force, Lenin is the justification most frequently appealed to, and each of them claims to be transmitting his true doctrine.

Generally speaking, the newer authoritarian Leninists, from Mao to Castro, have moved in the direction of greater subjectivity—extending even further Lenin's own shift from Marx. In his revolution Mao retained the traditional party scheme, but (in practice at least) relied on temporarily exploiting the desires of the wrong class—the peasantry. His more recent development has been to disrupt the Party proper, seen as an ossifying hindrance to the further imposition of willed change. As for Castro, he came to power without a party properly speaking, and with virtually no appeal to the masses, by means of guerrilla bands consisting almost entirely of free-lance revolutionaries; he then created a party machine of sorts, but the true conveyor belts of willed change are the workers' militia and direct television harangues.

These appear as "left" deviations from classical Marxism or even from classical Leninism. All the same, they retain at least that essential of the Lenin concept, the idea of transforming society from above by authoritarian means.

It is understandable that "liberal" Communists (and one section of the "liberal" opposition in the U.S.S.R.) also wish to enroll Lenin on their side. Obvious motives both of tactics and of *pietas* tend that way. And if the ploy helps Communists to evolve toward democracy by providing them with scriptural justification, there is something to be said for it, pragmatically speaking.

As an interpretation of Lenin's real teaching, it has a certain lack of substance. For example, Ernst Fischer, until recently a leader of the Austrian Communist Party, relies on quotations from Lenin to prove that he favored freedom of the press: but these are merely the promises Lenin made immediately after the seizure of power, to the effect that the temporary suppression of opposition newspapers would be lifted within weeks— the merest tactical bluff of the moment and no more fulfilled or intended to be fulfilled than the simultaneous promise to accept the decisions even of a hostile Constituent Assembly. And similarly with Fischer's claim that Lenin was eager for a genuine coalition government.

An argument rather less difficult to sustain than that presenting Lenin as a "liberal" in his own time is to say that things have changed, and Lenin would have changed his views accordingly. The Italian Communist weekly *Rinascità*, for example, suggests that *Imperialism* has been superseded. More crucial still to traditional Leninism is the question of the centralized party. The most usual thing here is to avoid referring to Lenin and rather to quote other Marxist texts, as the Italian Communist historian Ernesto Ragionieri quotes Engels to the effect that strong centralization and rigid discipline were necessary only "for a small party just starting out"; or to condemn the one-party system as, in the words of the French Communist *France Nouvelle*, "Stalin's old sectarian thesis."

On the other hand, Roger Garaudy, in his little philosophical *Lénine* (published before his expulsion even from the Politburo of the French Communist Party), argued flatly against *What Is to Be Done?*, claiming that Lenin had been misled by Kautsky, that he had later rehabilitated the initiative of the masses to some extent, and that in any case the doctrine was not a matter of principle but merely a tactic for Tsarist conditions. (The French Communists condemned his view and fully endorsed *What Is to Be Done?*)

The more usual course for "liberal" Communists seems to be to use the idea of a "liberal" Lenin as a stepping stone in their evolution to a broader view, such as that expressed by Garaudy's colleague, André Barionet, until 1968 director of the Center of Economic Studies of the French Communist Party. He now argues that "the October revolution in Russia had two courses before it: to rely on the Soviets and foster the creative initiative of the masses, or to rely on the Communist Party, which was to be increasingly stratified, disciplined, hierarchical, and ruled by an all-powerful bureaucracy controlling not only the State but all mass organizations and associations, including the Soviets themselves. This second course, of which Stalin is and will remain the symbol, was in fact chosen by Lenin himself."

Here a Communist has approached the view of a radical Social Democrat, the writer Günter Grass. Grass is dealing with, as it were, the opposite phenomenon, a Lenin who has been made attractive to some of the New Left by being acquitted of his authoritarian responsibilities:

> However critical the New Left imagines itself to be, it keeps going uncritically back to the concept of Marxism-Leninism, which is a contradiction in itself. The correct concept would have to be Leninism-Stalinism. The break from Marxism came with Lenin. . . . To make a genuine start with de-Staliniza-tion, the first sacrifice would have to be Lenin. If there had been no Lenin and no single-party system, if the separate Soviet Republics hadn't been deprived of all power, there could have been no Stalin.

When that has been said, how are we to sum up? In a most interesting and striking passage, Professor Mac-Intyre, while granting Lenin general responsibility for the Stalin regime, suggests that "those for whom the whole project of the new revolutionary liberation of mankind from exploitation and alienation is an absurd fantasy" are to some extent disqualified from writing about him. (Since MacIntyre concedes that the same considerations must prevent Gibbon from writing eccle-siastical history, the disqualification is scarcely a severe one.) But MacIntyre's phrasing seems misleading. One may believe in the possibility of such "liberation" while being skeptical about the "revolutionary" short-cut. (Nor need we be caught up in the parochialism of thinking that because the present period is, to a certain degree, revolutionary, this must inevitably persist. As Professor J. H. Plumb has written, "Historians too often think of rapid social change as creating conditions of turbulence; but societies can move as quickly into stability as into revolution, and between 1688 and 1725 Britain did just that.") More important, "absurd fantasy" implies contempt and amusement. A phrase like "dangerous delusion" would be better, and one reason why such a view is widely held is the very progress and results of Lenin's own revolution. Granting the purity of Lenin's motives, the most charitable critic is still entitled to feel that his career, if it does not prove, at least provides further evidence toward establishing that *le mieux est l'ennemi du bien.*

The other qualifications MacIntyre suggests as important in writing about Lenin are "a sense of scale" and "a sense of tragedy." One sees his point, though this short book is a work of exposition rather than of drama. Doubtless I have not given enough of the sheer scope of the events, the grandeur of the spectacle. We need not be immune to such sentiments to feel that, nevertheless, there is a certain vulgarity in accepting the role of spectator at some vast gladiatorial show.

It is, of course, true that there is something impressive about schemes for changing the entire world and in the actual transformation of a vast section of it. It is less obvious that persons who are historically on the grand scale should claim any sort of immunity to, or even toning down of, judgment and criticism simply on that account. To Napoleon's remark that power is never ridiculous, we may counterpose an English comment— Lytton Strachey's on Frederick the Great, that the results of arbitrary government "are apt to be disgraceful and absurd." One may recall, too, the context of Acton's famous remarks to Creighton on power and corruption: "You say that people in authority are not to be snubbed or sneered at from our pinnacle of conscious rectitude. I really don't know whether you exempt them because of their rank, or of their success and power, or of their date. . . ."

Having said which, it remains true that even to his severest critics Lenin may appear as a figure of a certain grandeur—as Lucifer appeared to Milton, caught up only in the major sin of extreme intellectual pride and lacking the pettier and more contemptible vices.

In a general way, that is. For as with all real originals of the hero or demon figures of historical myth, the real Lenin was not without lesser blemishes. As we have seen, opinions about him, among those who knew him well and those who met him briefly, vary between finding him attractive and repulsive. There are those who found him humane and broad-minded, regretfully forced to unpleasant acts. There are others who saw him as a monomaniacal hater quite unconcerned with morality and bent on the physical destruction of his enemies.

Djilas remarks that "All in all, Stalin was a monster who, while adhering to abstract, absolute, and fundamentally utopian ideas, in practice had no criterion but success—and this meant violence, and physical and spiritual extermination." There does seem to be a sense in which such a comment would not be wholly inapplicable to Lenin too. Of course, if we speak of him as a "monster" it cannot be in the same sense as Stalin. We may think rather in terms of *corruptio optimi pessima*, while feeling that Stalin had little of the best in him to corrupt. If, in Lenin's case, we take the word "monster" without these implications of horror, in its more basic sense of something exaggerated beyond reasonable norms, an enormous overgrowth of dogmatic certainty and concentrated will power, we may surely speak of him, in Chernyshevsky's way, as a monster.

Persecutors are almost always sincere. Nor are men who in given circumstances practice the opposite of what they preach necessarily hypocrites. Partly for lack of evidence, partly for lack of belief in the accuracy sometimes claimed for psychological interpretations, we have made little attempt to "go behind" Lenin's sincerity to discover what, if any, were his unconscious motivations. It is clear, indeed (for example, from his account of his quarrel with Plekhanov), that he had a turbulent, emotional heart. The full-time revolutionary who, as Axelrod rather exaggeratedly put it, "for twenty-four hours of the day is taken up with the revolution, who has no other thoughts but thoughts of the revolution, and who, even in his sleep, dreams of nothing but revolution," was, after all, a human being; and such holy simplicities do not grow in real flesh.

George Orwell remarks that the Russian Communists "never had the courage to recognize their own motives. They pretended, perhaps they even believed, that they had seized power unwillingly and for a limited time, and that just round the corner there lay a paradise where human beings would be free and equal." Their real or unconscious motive, he concludes, was power: "Power is not a means, it is an end."

The drive for power, the urge to manipulate the raw material of humanity, was certainly there. But in the last analysis, our main concern must be not a subjective estimate of motivation, but the judgment we make on the revolution Lenin carried out in Russia and the similar revolutions he planned for the rest of us.

Perhaps it will be appropriate to quote two Russians, one living and one fictional, on such revolutions: Alexander Solzhenitsyn in *Cancer Ward* has his sympathetic character Shulubin say, "Nor can you have socialism that's always banging on about hatred, because social life cannot be built on hatred. After a man has burned with hatred year in, year out, he simply can't announce one fine day, 'That's enough! As from today I'm finished with hatred, from now on I'm going to love!' No, if he's used to hating he'll go on hating." Or to put it another way, terror builds up its own traditions, institutions, cadres, and habits of mind, and the whole conception of creating a Good Society by authoritarian means contains a basic flaw.

From the opposite pole—that is, from not an ethical but a purely utilitarian point of view—another Soviet liberal has put the case against revolution in the West; Academician Andrei Sakharov, the most prominent Soviet scientist of the new generation, argues that—*even* apart from the possibility that a revolution would produce a Stalin, and *even* not taking into account the bloodshed of revolution itself—a revolution in the Western countries "does not appear to be an economically advantageous move for the working people," the advantage which was its orginal justification and motive.

Those who have had lifelong experience of the Leninist revolutionary state seem more inclined to see its defects than many in the West who are aware of the perhaps lesser, but no less hated, imperfections of their own countries and seek a rapid and effective means of dealing with them. The appeal of Leninism remains great, and—outside the Communist countries at least—it clearly resides in the attitude (not indeed a new one in history) that political and social transformation can be effected by will power and organization: that it is unnecessary to wait for the long and tedious "objective" social fermentation foreseen by the classical Marxists, let alone any makeshift "gradualism" or "meliorism." It is true enough that transformations can be effected. The point at issue is rather that the results may differ from theory, even to the extent that, after very great sacrifice, the last state of things is worse than the first.

Each new experiment hopes to have eliminated the troubles of the previous model, to have ensured that this time all will be well. Confidence in these attitudes must be shaken when we note that the precursors were equally convinced. As far as Lenin personally is concerned, it would doubtless be asking too much to think that a man of enormous talent and will power, who had devoted them to a single end over an entire adult lifetime, should in addition have had in his fifties the breadth and scope to judge the inadequacy of his theories and make a new start. Equally, it would be reprehensible for later generations not to learn from his experiences.

Politically speaking, in one view, Lenin is seen as a great surgeon of society coolly carrying out the necessary operations and amputations which the fainter-hearted would have mistakenly tried to avoid, with fatal results. The objection to this analogy would be that medical science is established on a considerably firmer basis than social science, and that Lenin might be thought to have been employing a theory of the anatomy and pathology of society which had been insufficiently tested—and was to prove inadequate.

As for his present effect, on a world scale, perhaps we may sum up along the following lines. The success and prestige of the Russian Revolution imposed on a great section of the world's left a doctrine of irreconcilability, of the division of opinions, movements, and states into those conducted on principles of truth and rectitude, and all the others in outer darkness. Whether one believes it to be a good thing or not, one must accept as part of Lenin's legacy not so much the divisions of the present world as the doctrinal element of irreconcilability which can be seen today both on the nuclear scale and in the small guerilla battle.

Macaulay remarks of an earlier revolutionary, John Hampden, that "Others could conquer: he alone could reconcile." Whether or not we feel such reconciliation to be desirable or even possible in the present world, we can at least be clear that Lenin and Leninism stand rather for conflict.

SHORT BIBLIOGRAPHY

An enormous number of books about Lenin are in existence. His own *Collected Works* (my references, unless otherwise stated, are to the third Russian edition) are for the specialist. The shorter *Selected Works* (New York: International Publishers, 1945), while indispensable to the serious student, contain a great deal of ephemeral factional argument, though this is often illustrative of Lenin's methods and attitudes. The most important texts of a more basic nature are: *What Is to Be Done?*; *Imperialism*; *State and Revolution*; and *Left-Wing Communism: an Infantile Disorder*— all to be found in the "Little Lenin Library" (New York: International Publishers) and included in many collections.

Of the many books on Lenin the most penetrating first-hand accounts are *Encounters with Lenin* by Nikolay Valentinov, translated by Paul Rosta and Brian Schapiro (New York: Oxford, 1968) and *Impressions of Lenin* by Angelica Balabanoff, translated by Isotta Cesari (Ann Arbor: University of Michigan, 1964).

The best accounts of Lenin's career are *The Bolsheviks* by Adam B. Ulam (New York: Macmillan, 1965); *Lenin* by David Shub (revised edition, London: Penguin, 1966; abridged edition, New York: New American Library); and *Three Who Made a Revolution: a Biographical History* by Bertram D. Wolfe (New York: Dial, 1948). The last, dealing also with Trotsky and Stalin, covers only the pre-revolutionary period.

The most interesting pieces critical of Lenin from a Marxist viewpoint are those of Rosa Luxemburg, published together as *The Russian Revolution* and *Leninism and Marxism* (Ann Arbor: University of Michigan, 1961). For Lenin's early career and for the formation of his political character, Richard Pipes' *Social Democracy and the St. Petersburg Labor Movement, 1885–1897* (Cambridge, Mass.: Harvard, 1963) is indispensable.

The best conspectus of Communist Party history, which up to 1920 is very largely that of Lenin and his decisions, is *The Communist Party of the Soviet Union* by Leonard Schapiro (New York: Random House, 1960). For the period 1917–1922 see the same author's *The Origins of Communist Autocracy* (Cambridge, Mass.: Harvard, 1955). Lenin himself regarded *The Russian Revolution, 1917*, by the Menshevik N. N. Sukhanov (New York: Oxford, 1955) as a particularly valuable record of the period.

The best account of the Revolution and the post-revolutionary period from the moderate socialist point of view is *The Soviet Revolution, 1917–1939* by Raphael R. Abramovitch (New York: International Universities, 1962).

Lenin: the Man, the Theorist, the Leader, edited by Leonard Schapiro and Peter Reddaway (New York: Praeger, 1967), is a most useful collection of essays (see, in particular, Peter Reddaway on Lenin's attitude to the arts and Alec Nove on Lenin as an economist).

The interesting essay by Alisdair MacIntyre quoted in the text is to be found in his *Against the Self-Images of the Age: Essays on Ideology and Philosophy* (New York: Schocken, 1971).

For Soviet accounts less purely hagiological than usual, see V. I. *Lenin in Petrograd and Moscow, 1917–1920* by Vladimir Bonch-Bruyevich and *Pages from Lenin's Life* by Lydia Fotieva (English-language edition, Moscow, 1960). *Lenin* by Leon Trotsky (New York, 1925) is of interest.

INDEX